WILLIAM BLOOM

Feeling Safe

How to be strong and positive in a changing world

PIATKUS

For Sophie and Sabrina

✿ *Visit the Piatkus website!*

Piatkus publishes a wide range of best-selling fiction and non-fiction, including books on health, mind, body & spirit, sex, self-help, cookery, biography and the paranormal.

If you want to:

- read descriptions of our popular titles
- buy our books over the Internet
- take advantage of our special offers
- enter our monthly competition
- learn more about your favourite Piatkus authors

VISIT OUR WEBSITE AT: www.piatkus.co.uk

Contents

1. The Need for Safety – *Recognising that feeling safe is the foundation of true success and personal development*   1

2. The Ingredients of Safety – *Understanding the biological, attitudinal and energetic map*   16

3. Managing Your Internal Chemistry – *Building up a reservoir of positive feelings for use in future challenges*   29

4. Generosity, Chivalry and Kindness – *Using care and a positive vision so that you and others feel safe*   48

5. The Invisible Dynamics of Safety – *Managing the energies, vibrations and atmospheres that can affect you*   67

6. Creating Energetic Protection – *Keeping your energy field centred and strong in disturbing circumstances*   97

7. The Power of Facing Reality – *Revealing and taming the hidden daemons that can destroy security*   115

8. A Safe and Great Soul – *Moving on from safety to fulfilment*   134

Resources   156

1
The Need for Safety

Recognising that feeling safe is the foundation of true success and personal development

You may be familiar with the experiments in which baby monkeys were removed from their mothers shortly after birth. They were given the best possible food and nutrients, and kept in a perfect temperature. But they were left alone most of the time, cut off from the warmth and nurture of their mothers and families.

These little creatures did not develop well. Their traumatic beginning affected the whole of their lives. They were uncertain of themselves and easily frightened. Their big, lost eyes were haunted with a need for reassuring comfort. They suffered mood swings, their behaviour moving between timid and aggressive. They had great difficulty fitting into their society.

Feeling insecure, these monkeys were unable to develop normally. It is the same with people when they lack the foundation of physical and psychological security.

Have you looked in someone's eyes when they are frightened or anxious? When people are traumatised and shocked, they are diminished. Watch people emerging from a tragic crash or disaster. They are smaller, frail, bewildered.

On a less dramatic scale, look into the eyes of someone who has just been rejected or not achieved what they wanted or expected. I once watched a businessman coping with the loss of a deal that he had worked on for many months. His jaw jutted, his shoulders were pulled back, he strutted and he was aggressive. But his eyes were wide and defensive. Psychologically, he had temporarily collapsed and a little boy who had lost his security blanket was revealed beneath all the macho wheeling and dealing.

When people experience a lack of safety – no matter what front they present to the world – they are unable to deal effectively with life. Something collapses within them. Watch a child frightened by a bully, or an adult sensing that a party, bar or night club is not his place; they too will shrink. Workers faced with information overload are reduced from confident and creative productivity to a frozen inertia. A tourist enters an historic place that has a forbidding and haunted atmosphere, and he too will stop uncertain whether to move forward. Some people can sense a wave of dread as a global political situation moves towards awful conflict. People who are abused and traumatised literally shrink and freeze.

The world is not a safe place, so what is the best way to handle it? The answer surely is to build up your own inner sense of safety. In this way, no matter what is happening around you, you have a stable base from which to operate.

When people have this core sense of safety, they feel confident and good, able to move with freedom and a positive attitude. Happy, truly successful and fulfilled people feel safe. They are able to handle the challenges and crises of life, and they are a supportive and encouraging blessing to the people around them.

The whole of this book is dedicated to helping you build that enduring and authentic state within yourself.

The Foundation of Personal Development

Feeling safe is one of the foundations of a normal, happy and fulfilling life. You simply cannot get on with the basic business of living if you feel insecure, frightened or anxious.

People need shelter, food and clothing just as a starting point for their security. It is tragically obvious that you cannot begin to grow into your full potential if you are worried about where the next meal is coming from or if you and your family might die. Those who live in war, famine and disaster zones, or in dangerous societies, have no choice but to give all their energy to the stark reality of survival.

Worse, some people have been so injured that they have nothing to focus on except their own wounds and trauma. They have neither the time nor the resources for the more profound purposes of human life – the search for meaning and fulfilment, spiritual growth, personal development, love and the bettering of the human and global condition.

But fear, anxiety and trauma are not only created by *physical* threat. People also need a core of *psychological* security. If, for example, you feel that you have no acceptable social identity, this can be as threatening as having a gun held to your head. This is not a shallow affair. When some people lose their jobs or their money or their status, they prefer to end their lives than exist without their previous sense of identity. They would rather die than lose their status. Whenever there is a financial slump, suicides increase. Men with families and good physical health die. People with no inner foundation collapse into shame and confusion.

Then there is the psychological threat that comes from being the target of prejudice – an outsider. It is impossible to feel safe when the people with whom you live and work do not accept you. It is exhausting and debilitating. To the target of prejudice – because of race or gender or disability – hostility and threat are always there, seen and unseen.

A feeling of safety is the natural bedrock of a human being's healthy development. Without that safety, there is ongoing nervousness – conscious and unconscious – and your ongoing behaviour can be hijacked, for example, by deep personality traits of bombast or victimisation. Bullies and braggarts are always psychologically insecure, as are those who whinge or manipulate. Without a sense of safety, there is no vitality or fuel for balanced growth and success. Your energy drains away because of endless tension and having to maintain postures of aggression or defence.

Even when people achieve material success and social status, there is no guarantee that they will lose their tension and find psychological security. According to recent research, materialistically successful people, for example, experience more nightmares than less driven folk. Accumulating wealth, possessions and power may create more threat and anxiety for an insecure person who has a need to control – there is just more stuff now to regulate. Look at the control freaks you know. Be aware of your own need to control. Its source is a lack of inner safety.

Success often camouflages fear and, even worse, stimulates feelings of anxiety. Moreover, powerful physical protection may not improve the situation. Fortresses, castles, weapons, bodyguards, and all the martial and self-defence arts do not make insecure people feel secure.

The world is a dangerous place in too many ways. And people are insecure in so many ways.

The purpose of this book is to help everyone develop an authentic internal sense of safety regardless of life circumstances – whether they are rich or poor, high or low in status, or live in peace or in conflict. This kind of internal security comes from an inner strength and wisdom. It is a permanent part of your character. It is also a positive trait for the community around you, and makes other people feel safe, too. It is great to have neighbours, colleagues and friends who are solid. They are the ones we turn to in a crisis.

On the streets, if someone is called 'safe' it is a sign of approval and acceptance. It means that person is cool and has a positive presence. The safe person stays calm and intelligent – and knows when and when not to act. You are cool, but not coldly detached. Observant, but not a hostile witness. You do not stand by when someone is being bullied or hurt. Your presence has strength, even warmth. There is something about you that is watchful, careful and encouraging. You are good to have around.

The Ingredients of Inner Safety

This book will give you some essential but simple strategies and ideas for how to achieve inner safety. In the same way that water flows down to the sea, feeling secure and confident is how human beings are meant to be. These feelings are built into people and my experience is that everyone can achieve them, regardless of their history or circumstances.

I have researched, developed and taught these strategies for almost thirty years to many different types of people, supporting their development. At the beginning, my interest was almost purely personal as I developed my own psychological and physical security. I experienced all this directly when I was a young man. In my early twenties, I used to ride with a motorbike gang and in my late twenties, I managed one of the roughest pubs in my town for a while.

I knew nothing then about body chemistry, but the range of feelings I experienced when danger was around fascinated me. When something perilous started, I could feel my body begin to pump out adrenaline and I would begin to lose control, going spontaneously into feelings of tension and agitation. I could not look people in the eye. I radiated anxiety. Others noticed this and knew I was vulnerable. In order to stay safe, I had to control my adrenaline.

Using strategies from meditation and the martial arts, I learned to guide my attitude and my body into feeling calm and strong.

I then became interested in the social and political implications surrounding this issue, and completed doctoral research into how individual issues of personal security spilled over into the world community; for a while I taught Psychological Problems in International Politics at university. I then became more interested in a hands-on approach and worked for ten years in an inner city community college with special needs adults and adolescents, many of whom were deep in trauma and anxiety.

My work developed in a more holistic way, integrating information from contemporary medical science, psychology, meditation and the martial arts – providing the ingredients that go into the recipe for feeling safe.

Alongside my writing and public courses I now also work with, among others, embassy staff and palliative care nurses, men and women at the coal face of crisis and danger. Like you, these people need to be fully aware of all life's realities and at the same time feel secure and confident.

In this book I will share with you the strategies for feeling safe that I know are effective and that I have seen work time and time again. They include:

- Managing the hormones of safety and fear.

- Building a reservoir of positive feelings for use in future crises.

- Staying connected to the good things in life regardless of the challenging circumstances.

- Managing your energy and creating clear boundaries.

- Building inner strength.

- Developing courage and chivalry.

- Looking at the things you do not like.

- Staying calm and strong when facing provocation.

- Being larger than the issue.

- Creating atmospheres and attitudes that encourage others.

None of these is difficult to practise if you follow the ideas and techniques in the following chapters. Doing so will allow you to maintain a genuine attitude of stability, enjoyment and generosity in situations that might previously have disturbed you: oppressive family, disgruntled colleagues, surly students, rude clients, information overload, negative atmospheres, deadlines, personal and political crisis – in fact, all the stuff that makes for a difficult life. You may still get angry, tense or upset, but there will be a stable core to which you can always return.

These techniques will also support and help you if you have the misfortune to suffer more extreme situations of danger, threat and injury. My greatest wish is, of course, that neither you nor any other living being will ever experience abuse or terror and that if – God forbid – this were to happen, you would be surrounded by an abundance of effective carers, healers and friends. This book will, however, also help to prepare you for any such situations of dramatic change and danger.

The Need for this Basic Life Skill

The ability to *feel safe whatever the external circumstances* is a crucial life skill that is especially needed in the modern world.

It is not just threats of physical violence that you may encounter. You live in an age when tension and anxiety are considered normal. Everything is humming, buzzing and vibrating with change. Change means new things and an endless succession of new things creates tension. You can never relax in the knowledge that you now know enough.

Never before has humanity experienced such a relentless stream of shift, threat and stimulation. In the past, you could fall asleep on a village green and wake up a hundred years later and the place would be largely the same. Same green fields, same buildings, same tracks, same pond. Today, you live in a tidal wave of endless and accelerating transformation. Nothing is permanent or safe. The last fifty years have seen more change on the planet than the 5,000 years that came before.

You have to be a life-long learner because the world is continuously altering and making new demands upon you. Each day can feel like an examination in whether you are up to date with what you need to know now. The old kinds of security – a job for life, stable local community, consistent morality and ethics, respect for age and authority – have gone. From month to month we simply do not know if our careers are safe. Corporations and trades that previously seemed impregnable suddenly shake and fall. Humming consistently in the background of our lives is concern over whether we will be able to continue to pay the rent or mortgage. Decades of investment in safe pension schemes can disappear overnight, transforming people's expectations and hopes for the last years of their lives.

And then there is the 'noise' – the throbbing and electric momentum of the modern world, which is pricking at you with a never-ending intensity.

You are probably so accustomed to all this that you are not consciously bothered by it. But, below your threshold of awareness, your senses are fully aware of it. You simply filter out the information that does not seem important. From the day you were born, you were subject to the input of mechanical and electronic stuff. It may seem normal. It may even seem partly enjoyable. But it is harsh to the senses. The growl and smell of traffic. The endless sound and images from the media. The stark glare of electric lighting. The radiation from computer and other screens. The microwave frequencies of mobile phones and transmitters. The list is endless.

We love these things. We take them for granted. But when did you last sleep in a place where there was no electricity and no hum of traffic? The calm is fantastic. Compare your local high street, office or kitchen with the experience of moonlight on an ocean, of lying on a beach, of walking in mountains!

Rapid change has also hit how we manage our relationships. There is a huge freedom today that was not available or allowed a few decades ago. Barely a century ago premarital sex was rare or scorned; today – at least in the West – that is laughable in most quarters. The idea of the sanctity of a woman's virginity is not even part of the modern landscape. Sexual freedom, considered the cutting edge of radical change a few decades ago, is now normal. Some relationships last; others don't. We seem to have accepted the reality that all marriages may fail and that the ones that endure may even be peculiar.

Human beings were not biologically designed to handle all this stimulation. *Stop the world I want to get off* was the title of a pop song in the 1950s. What would the singer make of the twenty-first century?

The freedom is great and wonderful, but beneath it all there is a psychological cost. It is difficult to find the emotional stability that will make us feel safe and stable.

Walking through central London one day, I saw this woman's tight sleeveless pink T-shirt on which were written the words: *Faster Faster Kill Kill Kill.* It amused and concerned me.

I do not want to poop the party. I just want you to be realistic. The last decades have been exciting and highly enjoyable for most people. There has been a lot of action. It has engrossed our culture. But beneath it all you are still just a human being, flesh and blood, a complex and very sophisticated mammal with certain instincts and needs. At one level you are having a party. At another, unconscious level, there is tension. Beneath all the newness and jazz, there is too much stimulation and speedy change. You are probably hyped up and living with subliminal tension. It is easiest to pretend it does not exist.

But the unconscious level does surface – with a vengeance. The underlying tension slowly or suddenly emerges in physical and psychological distress – backache, headache, road rage, violence, depression, burnout, stomach ulcers, strokes and so on. The majority of illnesses when you are past thirty years old derive from some kind of tension constricting what should be a free-flowing circulation of blood, breath and hormones.

External realities also intrude – with a vengeance. Naturally, people do not want to look carefully at frightening stuff, but the cost of not looking is too high. Perhaps the greatest wound to the United States and the Western world on 11 September 2001 was the mass psychological trauma when the illusion of security was shattered. It had all seemed so safe, but overnight the great castle of safety had been penetrated and nobody was secure.

For all the immense success in prolonging life, making childbirth safe, bringing hygiene into daily life and developing modern medicine, we are still faced with terrible scourges, such as the threat of nuclear and biochemical weapons, environmental catastrophe or AIDs. You may walk happily down to the shopping centre, but there is always the very real possibility of danger.

It is childish and psychologically unhealthy to pretend that life is safe, because beneath the pretence, you know full well that there are dangers. Stability and safety are an illusion. Life is full of tragedy. The forces of nature can shock and destroy anything through earthquakes, storms, tornadoes, drought and pestilence. Illness and death can come suddenly to you or your loved ones. Stable relationships that you expected to endure may be betrayed. Political and commercial situations can transform overnight. Financial success can turn to ruin. The mugger, the fascist and the terrorist lurk in the shadows.

Dare to look at reality and you will see that you cannot depend on the dependable. Life is not safe. People have never been able to control their circumstances. You can spend the whole of your life building pleasurable and secure surroundings, but they may suddenly be destroyed by factors completely beyond your control.

This book is fully realistic about all that and its strategies will show you how to look at life's unpleasant realities – and at the same time to feel secure, strong and confident.

Becoming Strong and Confident

So, how do you become truly safe? I believe it is natural for people to be secure and confident if they follow some simple guidelines.

There are models of this kind of inner strength all around us. What do good parents, managers, friends, teachers, leaders, colleagues and martial artists have in common? They know how to be strong, optimistic and watchful at times of crisis. Somewhere in your life, perhaps in your family or your schooling, at work or in sport, you surely know people who carry this attitude.

One of my first jobs was in a large publishing company and I remember two people clearly. One was the woman who brought around the tea trolley – this was before the coffee machine. The other was one of the directors. When the tea lady came around, everyone cheered up. Even the testiest and most irritated staff would relax as she dispensed the beverages and biscuits. If someone was in a filthy mood, she would eye him carefully before deciding whether to crack a joke or move on. There was a certain natural wisdom about her. Unflappable.

The director was also like that. He had to make significant and difficult decisions. He often needed to say 'no', but he always maintained a friendly dignity. Occasionally I sat in on board meetings that went on too long and were filled with frayed nerves. The director always held himself steady, even when aggressively challenged. Again, unflappable.

But what also distinguished these two people was a warmth of character, which they unconsciously radiated. When there was trouble, the radiation was amplified. When there was a crisis, they were especially strong and encouraging. They made others feel safe.

Just like these people, there are many others who remain strong and positive in genuinely terrible situations. Surrounded by true terror and hardship, they maintain their good nature. You must know people like this. How did they get to be that way? Perhaps scientists will discover a gene of unflappability and generous courage, but I doubt it.

Good martial artists also know all about this. The greatest fighters are those who do not fight and have no need to fight. They emanate a sense of safety that 'disarms' their opponents. They feel so safe within themselves that they never attract the events that might lead to conflict.

Faced by a thousand enemies, the martial artist can stand facing them, feeling totally secure and calm. He can see, feel and hear everything. He knows he may even die, but his inner stability is so great and so genuine that he maintains his calm happiness. You too can develop that inner equilibrium.

On a freezing dark winter evening on the outskirts of London, I once watched a seven months pregnant American woman demonstrating that equilibrium as she walked across the car park and into the building where she was about to meet the examiner for her British driving test. She was nervous about driving on the left and her anxiety had been building. Nevertheless, before the examination, she steadied herself fully. She paused before entering the office and turned briefly to look at me. She raised her fist high in the air and shouted a phrase used by Native Americans before they went into battle. Her voice echoed across the tarmac, 'Today is a good day to die!'

I laughed and was impressed by her attitude. She had fully managed her internal chemistry when it was required. Needless to say, she passed the test.

I am not saying that taking a driving test is the same as handling abuse or terror, but there are similarities in how people feel and behave in those situations. When working with embassy staff, for example, I was disarmed by how honest they sometimes were about their feelings and their talents. Many admitted that they could more easily handle a terrorist attack than a difficult teenager or domineering parent or boss. Different people are sensitive to different forms of threat.

Maintaining a strong and philanthropic attitude in difficult situations is a character trait – it seems that some people are born with it – but it is also an acquired skill that can be learnt and transferred to different situations. The strategies and concepts of *Feeling Safe* are simple, natural and easy to put into practice. I have seen many people succeed with them.

One handsome man I knew had enhanced his physique with bodybuilding and looked great. But he was, in fact, lost in a neurotic relationship and a career that depressed him. His inability to manage insecurity and threat made him a victim who was unable to manage and guide his life. Yet he learned how to make himself feel safe and developed a stronger centre. From this new starting point, he was able to liberate himself and his partner from their loop of anger and distress, and he had the courage to follow his passion into a new career.

A woman who held a very senior role in a training organisation became disgusted at the political infighting, egoism and conflict at the top of the organisation. The source of all of it was the man who had started and still ran the outfit. For three years she stewed in uncomfortable and tense indecision, insecure and anxious about what to do. She swung between keeping her head down and complaining, and erupting into frustrated rudeness.

Following the concepts of *Feeling Safe*, this woman too found a new composure and ability to look more clearly at the whole situation. With dignity, resolution and some courage, she set about transforming the organisation and negotiating with the boss. As it turned out, he could not be moved and the other senior executives were also entrenched in their positions. With no regrets or rancour, having done her best, the woman moved on to new fields where she was indeed able to do her best.

And I must be honest. In my own life too these strategies have been hugely important in bringing me happiness and, on my terms, the success I want. I hope they do the same for you.

2
The Ingredients of Safety

Understanding the biological, attitudinal and energetic map

What does it really mean to feel safe?

For a start, it is not an idea in your head. It is not a concept that floats around out there as a good idea. If you feel safe, you FEEL it, in your body. It is physical. It is relaxed and comfortable, flexible and free, centred and strong.

Now look at the symptoms when people do not feel safe:

- Sweaty palms.

- Tense muscles.

- Gut ache.

- Dry mouth.

- Headache.

- Stiffness.

- Fidgeting.

- Anxious stomach and taut chest.

- Clenched fists.

- Stuttering.

- Butterflies in the stomach.

- Diarrhoea.

- Inability to move and partial paralysis.

- Blinking.

- Tears.

- Explosive tension.

- Exhaustion.

- Hairs prickling.

One or more of these symptoms can move through someone's body and can profoundly affect their mood and behaviour. There are many people, for example, who are usually fairly calm, but take them into an interview situation and they lose it. Unable to control themselves, desperately trying to stay dignified, they start sweating profusely, or their hands tremble, or their mouth dries up and their lips make strange smacking noises!

These unpleasant physical reactions can really influence you, dominating your moods, thoughts and how you behave. As the physical symptoms explode within your body, there is a knock-on emotional effect. You may start to feel aggressive, defensive, timid, frightened, self-pitying, victimised, angry, snide, sarcastic, scared, bombastic, evasive, suspicious and so on. There are people who go to see their bank managers, seeking a loan and ready with their sensible plan of action. But in the meeting they get so overwhelmed by their own uncontrollable physical sensations that they start to speak incoherently and then walk out backwards as if leaving the presence of some great monarch. One woman I knew got so nervous in formal situations that she once ended up sitting on a coffee table chain-smoking cocktail chips.

All of this can happen because of the chemistry and the sensations in your body. Unpleasant physical sensations cascade through your emotions and mind. This is why people take antidepressants – including alcohol and caffeine – to cheer themselves up. The narcotic changes their body chemistry. The body feels better. So emotions feel better. So the mind feels better. They smile again. But they are sitting on a load of stuff only temporarily anaesthetised.

I remember a very insecure man who started to feel wonderful taking the antidepressant Prozac. At one stage, in his new-found confidence, he decided to go bungee-jumping – he was overweight and fifty – and hurled himself off a high crane over the River Thames in central London. The cords were attached to his ankles, but instead of coming down headfirst like everyone else, he jumped feet first. He was whipped back up and down several times and it took many months for his bruised and dislocated spine to settle back into shape. He told me that he did it because it felt good at the time. The antidepressant had made him feel too safe – and unrealistic.

All of this underlines that feeling safe is grounded in the actual physical sensation. To experience fear and insecurity is to feel physical tension and anxiety. To experience safety and security is to feel physical relaxation and well-being.

If you feel truly safe you stay feeling good even when there is threat around you. Someone can be having a pop at you, you may be in crisis or danger, but your body stays relaxed and cool. And if your body stays comfortable, this provides the foundation for positive emotions and constructive thinking. You remain able to deliver your best – there is nothing inhibiting your performance.

Feeling safe is a flesh and blood issue. It is not academic.

Your Emotions and Mind Affect Your Body

It does not just begin in the body and then ripple out psychologically. It is a two-way process. Upset emotions or an overwhelmed mind affect your body chemistry. If, for example, you keep behaving in an emotionally and mentally intense way for an extended period – months or years – the likelihood is that this will ultimately create physical illness.

There are millions of people who are experiencing arthritis, rheumatism, strokes, stomach ulcers and so on, precisely because of the physical effects of long-term psychological tension.

In fact, one of the cutting edges of research in contemporary medical science involves mapping exactly how thoughts and moods affect body chemistry and health. The fields of neuro-science, endocrinology and psychology are merging – the discipline is called psychoneuroimmunology (PNP) – as medicine discovers the precise links between states of mind, emotional moods and physical chemistry.

Medieval European doctors were fully aware of this connection between physiological chemistry and a person's temperament. They described a person's general character as having a certain humour. The four primary humours were blood, phlegm, choler (yellow bile) and melancholy (black bile). For physical health these humours needed to be in balance. This was especially difficult if a person's psychological temperament was, for example, too melancholic. It was not the body that needed treating, but the personality.

This is also the approach of Eastern and holistic approaches to healthcare. The link between the mind and the body is absolutely crucial. Our psychological mood has a profound effect on our body chemistry and vice versa.

The Cauldron of Hormones

When you feel safe, your body is experiencing a completely different hormonal chemistry from when it feels threatened.

If you perceive a threat and feel frightened, your body automatically produces adrenaline and cortisol. Adrenaline is the hormone responsible for the rush of electric energy in response to a threat. People often say that it creates three physical options: flight, fright or fight. If the adrenaline is not burned up by some kind of activity, it freezes into tense fear. Cortisol is then the hormone that is instrumental in creating physical tension. Together, these two hormones can create a physical hell state. They become frozen in the body, creating ongoing feelings of tension and anxiety.

Many people know about this only too well and they live their whole lives with an ongoing background hum of tension and dread, occasionally peaking in panic attacks. To say the least, this is the opposite of feeling safe.

A calm, flexible and happy body, on the other hand, is enjoying a consistent flow of endorphins, the 'miracle hormones'. They are the body's natural morphine or opium and are responsible for feelings of pleasure and well-being, as well as killing pain and boosting the immune system. In a healthy person, endorphins are produced continuously and they provide a background chemistry that powerfully supports a good attitude and psychological health.

For the body to feel safe, the volume of cortisol and adrenaline needs to be turned down, and the volume of endorphins amplified. By looking after your body properly, by adopting the right emotional and mental attitudes, by using certain easy techniques, you can indeed manage your body's chemistry.

Imagine that your body is like a cauldron. Are you stewing in the freezing battery acid of tension or enjoying a warm bath of well-being? Is this cauldron filled with good or nasty things? What has life put in it? What has your own attitude put in it?

Compare the body language of a tense, angry, frustrated and vindictive person with that of someone who is generous, friendly, happy and relaxed. It is the cauldron of frozen battery acid versus the hot tub of comfortable well-being. Which do you choose?

Another aspect of true safety, then, is the ability to manage your internal chemistry.

The chemical state of your body – acidic tension or well-being – also affects other people. It is not just your behaviour and attitude, but also your scent or vibration, that comes into play here. It is recognised that dogs and other animals can smell fear. I am certain that human beings can also sense whether there is fear or security in you and that they respond accordingly. Your fear and tension can trigger the same in others. Equally, your safety and well-being feel good to those around you. Watch what happens in an office when a nasty senior manager walks into the room: everyone freezes.

Having Strength and Courage

When a lioness is playing with her cubs, you do not join in. The moment she senses the slightest threat to the cubs, she is prepared to kill to protect them. This too is what most human parents feel about their children.

Strength and courage are natural emotions for human beings. They lie dormant in you waiting for the situation that needs them. Most parents have experienced this. Perhaps its source is a genetic imperative that ensures the survival of the species.

Feeling safe, therefore, means more than just being calm in the face of danger. It also means that you are prepared to be strong, prepared to fight. You do not sit passively while children are threatened. You do something about it.

When there is danger, you need to be able to manifest the force and the roar of a lion. These are not in the first place the attributes of physical strength or an ability to physically fight. They are originally moral and emotional qualities. They belong to your character. In some people they are naturally strong. In others they need to be developed.

Again, in your life you know people who display this kind of fortitude. They do not cave in when there is loss or failure. One of the qualities that most inspires people about Mother Theresa or the Dalai Lama is that they demonstrate strength and courage without physically fighting. To be clear, though, they may be attitudinally aggressive. A tiny nun can possess a thousand times more emotional, psychological and moral strength than a 300-pound wrestler.

There is often a problem with stress management in that people learn how to relax, but not how to assert clear boundaries against abuse. People may walk all over you if you are too relaxed and yielding, which will only bring more stress and anxiety.

Occasionally you may need to intervene physically. What choice would you have if you saw your child – or any child – being abused? There are also times when you may need physically to push someone away from you. Of course, it is always a matter of personal judgement about whether such behaviour is appropriate or makes the situation worse. Nevertheless at certain times you need the life skill of physical courage.

Equally, you need the skill of emotional and moral strength when it is right and necessary. You need to be able to speak the truth in situations where others prefer silence.

So, the kind of safety that I want you to develop and experience includes the ability, when necessary, to be morally strong, courageous and secure.

Being Observant, Good Humoured and Kind to Yourself

People who feel safe are also distinguished by their ability to hold a slight distance from the passions and processes of the moment – even in a personal crisis. They are watchful, yet engaged and constructive. They are emotionally strong and relaxed.

Philosophers and martial artists alike have always taught the necessity of being watchful. Modern psychologists are also clear that an important part of mental health is the ability to detach and observe yourself and the world around you. This creates a psychological stability that underpins and calms your nervous and hormonal system.

It is impossible to create or maintain a sense of safety without the ability to observe yourself and have a sense of proportion about yourself. At one end of the spectrum is the drama-queen, lost in emotions and self-absorption, absolutely unable to manage the internal chemistry. At the other end is a well-balanced human being, able to monitor and manage their moods and chemistry. They can witness themselves with relaxed good humour.

This ability to observe life and your own behaviour with some detached mental clarity and kind humour is a fundamental life skill. With that one skill, you can create sanity for yourself. If you are lost in the incessant stimulation of a full life, lost in your own emotions and ambitions and drama, and always reacting to the events and activities around you, you will find it impossible to feel safe. It is a recipe for insecurity, anxiety and aggression.

A kind and observant mind can be the basis of safety. One of the problems with crisis, threat and ongoing internal drama is that you lose perspective. You forget where you really are. Your values become lost. You lose sight of the wonderful and good things in life. But switch on your kind and observant mind, separate yourself from all the overwhelming stimulation, and you can see the bigger picture. No matter how terrible life might seem, the wider perspective always has some beauty and humour.

If you are calm and watchful, you can create a mood of optimism and happiness, even enthusiasm, because when you turn your focus away from the endless buzz, you will always rediscover the good things of life. 'What use is that in a world tumbling into environmental or terrorist destruction?' you may ask. The answer is simple. You cannot be part of the solution if you are lost and overwhelmed by the problem. Connection to the good things of life brings hope and wisdom. 'What use is that,' you may again ask, 'if someone is in a situation of abuse or terror?' The answer again is simple. In terrible situations, it is precisely that attitude which may keep you sane and help you survive.

Over and over again, in situations of life or death, it is the person who retains a calm and optimistic disposition who endures and inspires others. If you go into a hospital emergency ward and watch the staff, who are the effective and efficient carers? Certainly not the pessimists or those flapping around like headless chickens. The successful carers are those who retain a sense of proportion and an awareness that goes beyond the immediate emergencies. God bless the ambulance staff and the rescuers who come into physical disasters with dignity, courage and immense good will.

If you are watchful and strongly connected to the good things of life, you can also develop a kind and accepting attitude towards all the troubles and negativity that you yourself may be experiencing. This is very important. There may come times when life's wounds take you into shock, anger and grief – feelings and emotions that are natural and part of everyone's healing process. But if you have developed the ability to be kind and caring towards yourself – not just towards others – then you will have created an inner space of sanity and safety to which you can return.

There are, for example, many people in the caring professions who are fantastic at looking after other people in a wise and supportive way. They are hopeless, however, at looking after themselves, and often finally burn out and collapse in nervous exhaustion. On the other hand, I know carers who stay cheerful and energetic all the way through their careers. What these people have in common is that they know how to look after themselves. They know when to pause and rest.

They know when it is time for an enjoyable treat. They look after themselves realistically.

Managing Your Energy Field

Another key feature of feeling safe is to have a strong energy field with clear boundaries. This may be a new concept to you if you are not familiar with holistic and Eastern medicine. Every living creature has a subtle energy body that is partly electromagnetic – think of a conga eel with its ability to give electric shocks – and partly made up of vitality, known as *prana* or *chi* in ayurvedic and taoist medicine. If your energy field – also sometimes known as your *aura* in the West – lacks vitality or leaks, you will be affected and depleted by other energies, atmospheres and vibrations.

A healthy body, generous emotions, a positive mental attitude and a connection to the good things of life will usually be enough to keep your energy field secure and impregnable. Nevertheless there may be times when you need more immediate strategies to deliberately strengthen your energy. In Chapters 5 and 6 you will pick up some key concepts and techniques for easily managing and reinforcing your field.

A strong energy field has significant health benefits. Many people know exactly what it is like to feel drained by people and situations. It is psychologically depressing and physically exhausting, not a recipe for feeling good.

There are also significant gains here for the people around you. As you yourself become energetically stronger and safer, so you radiate your safety to include others. If you feel safe and great, your presence can be a powerful gift to everyone around you. But just as the negative atmosphere of a person or place can adversely affect you, so your vibrations can influence other people. If your own nervous system is on overload and your field is deflated, it can suck the energy out of your companions or put them on edge. I have seen good teams deflated and lose their confident spirit through the presence of just one exhausted and bad-tempered member, even if that person has kept quiet.

I have trained people in managing these kinds of challenge for almost thirty years and I know that these problems are very real. Over and over, I meet good men and women who have been exhausted and sometimes overwhelmed by the vibrations of other people. I think immediately of an inner city teacher who retired early and took five years to recover from her burnout, and of an effective CEO who was in fact continually drained by the aggressive culture of his business.

If this talk about energy fields and vibrations is new to you, let me reassure you that this area is considered of core importance in holistic healthcare and Eastern medicine. Sensing energy fields is especially developed in many blind people and becomes a reliable sixth sense. But you do not have to be blind to sense when your children, partners or bosses are in a bad mood. The feeling can fill a whole building. Equally, not even the greatest sceptic of 'energies' would buy or rent a home that 'felt' bad. In fact, when looking for a new home, one of the first things that people notice is the property's atmosphere. You may also have the ability to walk into a bar and instinctively sense that violence is in the air and so steer yourself away in another direction.

Summary – the Ingredients for Feeling Safe

So there are many factors which work together to create a sense of inner safety, but the most important is the physical experience of feeling good and all right. This experience is rooted in your body chemistry. It is stable and it endures even when you are dealing with danger or a crisis. Your body remains feeling calm as you get on with the dangerous business of everyday life. This is the total opposite of the physical symptoms of anxiety, such as sweating and trembling.

This physical sense of well-being has a huge and positive influence in making you feel psychologically stable and good, too. Instead of losing your rag and getting lost in the chemicals of a sudden mood change, you can retain your composure, confidence and creativity. Events that used to trigger the chemicals of anxiety and the feelings of defence or hostility are now water off a duck's back.

But you have to remember that your mental and emotional states have a real effect on your body chemistry and they need to be managed. Psychological distress and destructive attitudes anchor down into your body, triggering the hormones of anxiety and building up reservoirs of tension. In the medium and long term, this can have debilitating effects on your physical and mental health.

People who feel safe are generous, strong and courageous, wanting to support and defend that which they value. In difficult times they keep a clear mind and are able to watch the ups and downs of life with good-natured detachment. Especially at times of crisis, they maintain a sense of proportion, keep an eye on the bigger picture and stay connected with the good things of life.

They also have a strong, calm energy field with clear boundaries. They seem to radiate an invisible quality that makes others feel safe, too. People who feel safe, feel good inside and are also a blessing to those around them.

3
Managing Your Internal Chemistry

Building up a reservoir of positive feelings for use in future challenges

When someone trembles, tenses or sweats in a crisis, a biochemical process is happening inside their body. People physically feel fear and tension because their bodies are filled with chemicals that create these distinct feelings. A panic attack or a more general background sense of tension has a chemical source.

In order to feel safe and to feel good, you must be able to steer your body away from producing the chemicals and hormones of fear, and towards actively stimulating the chemicals of feeling good. You need to be able to do this in a crisis and you also want it running continuously through your life.

Transforming the Old Fears

Your basic choice is between stewing in the frozen battery acid of adrenaline and cortisol – the hormones of fear and tension – or brewing happily in a hot tub of fluid confidence created by the hormones of well-being, called endorphins. The baby monkeys, deprived of their mothers, were condemned to a life of anxiety, their nervous and endocrine systems frozen with insecurity. Those who were given full nurture when young always maintained a certain contented equilibrium.

It is obviously easier to manage immediate challenges and anxieties if you have a reservoir of positive chemicals upon which you can draw. One of your goals, therefore, must be to create a long-term attitude and life-style that produces the chemistry of safety. You have to live in a body whose main chemical sensation is that of security, confidence and optimism. You have to empty out and transform the pockets of ancient anxiety, and replace them with positive chemical feelings.

Your first job, therefore, is to manage the chemistry of your body, and to do this it is necessary to be clear about your history. In what are you stewing? Although you may not be conscious of it, the cells in your body hold the tense and acidic chemical memories of past fears and traumas. When something frightened or disturbed you, your body instinctively went into an aggressive–defensive mode. Your muscles tensed as you prepared for some kind of remedial action. Unless you fully used up all that tension and adrenaline and then sank back into full relaxation, your body still retains some of the fear in its cellular memory. *Old crises live on in the chemistry of your cells.*

Watch a dog or cat when it has been frightened. Sooner or later it will give itself a thorough shake and shudder, burning up the adrenaline and releasing the tension. Then the animal will have a long stretch followed by a relaxed walk. Then it will stretch again and later curl up into a completely relaxed rest. The animal's instincts lead it to unloading the chemicals of fear.

You probably did not shudder like a dog every time you were frightened, then stretch and curl up – so the chemistry of the original fear still sits in your cells, haunting, sometimes growling or hissing. The hormones produced at the time of the original scare are still in the background. Your history of anxious times remains as a continuous background tension and it provides fertile ground for planting and growing new anxieties, irritations and anger.

There is a terrible vicious circle here. If you already carry the memories of tension, then you are much more likely to experience them again in a crisis – because they are always there *in you* ready to be triggered. You surely know, at its worst, paranoid and victimised people who unconsciously recreate their reality. I think of a mother who while waiting to pick up her child in the school playground always circulated among the other parents picking up and distributing worrying gossip. She did this in a conspiratorial and persecuted way, and with predictable regularity fell out with other parents, accusing them of being malicious. She was caught in a cycle of her own fearful chemistry.

Equally, I remember a confident and well-meaning local town councillor who was always seeing things in the best possible light. Even the folk in opposing political parties were pleased to see him and felt good when he was around. He was also a school governor and once, after an intense two-day process of interviewing for a new deputy head of the school, no appointment was actually made. The interviewing panel were exhausted, disappointed and irritable. 'Well,' he said cheerfully, 'that's the price of democracy. Worth it, isn't it?' The group cheered up. His basic chemistry was upbeat and positively influenced others.

It is crucial that any ancient negative chemistry you carry is melted, neutralised and transformed. You need to come out of the bath of frozen battery acid and sink into the hot tub of relaxation. If your natural opiates can come back in to flow through your whole body, then the old stuff will indeed have been healed and it will be virtually impossible for you to feel tension, anxiety and fear.

And here is some good news. It is very simple and easy to trigger the production of your natural opiates. Anything you find pleasurable produces them!

Pause and Detach

Think of some food you really like and your mouth will produce saliva. Think of your favourite sex object and you will also feel a response in your body. Whether you like it or not you are born with a biology that is programmed to react to certain triggers. Your mind must learn to manage these programmes of instinctive reaction.

This self-management is one of the major goals of educa-tion and self-development – the discipline and wisdom to override and guide your own biological drives. As a child you were guided and looked after by the older people around you. As you grew older, you became increasingly independent and developed your own mind. Your own mind is now the parent and guardian of your body. But how wisely or well does it manage your instincts? In one of the greatest Hindu religious texts, the *Bhagavad Ghita*, this process is likened to saddling and riding a wild horse. The rider is your soul.

As a human being your nervous system and your psychological reflexes are highly complex. Whatever you may seem like on the surface, inside you have a unique, rich and often painful history. Whoever you are, whatever your age or status, you have moods and reactions that are difficult to control. Certain types of people and certain types of behaviour evoke an involuntary response from you. Subconsciously people have extremely long memories.

You walk down a long, narrow alley at night and suddenly you see someone's shadow in the distance. Involuntarily you experience fear. But it is not the shadow that has triggered fear, it is your own mind. You get closer and the shadow turns out to be nothing.

At its most extreme you may become a prisoner, a victim of your own projections – seeing danger and threats where they do not actually exist. Because of your history, you may perceive everything through a lens of tension. You unconsciously project your inner anxiety on to everything in the world around you – your job, home, relationship, looks, belongings and so on. If something is not right in any of them, you become upset and feel emotional pain. You blame everything and have no understanding that the distress in fact begins in you. To one degree or another everyone does this sometimes, especially when stressed or exhausted.

This is a very powerful pattern. The unconscious memories of past injuries, your body chemistry, your mood and your mental state all combine to create a distressing life-style.

In Buddhism, there is a clear and useful piece of advice for managing all this: 'Everybody suffers. The issue is not the suffering. The issue is your mental attitude towards it.' When you feel depressed or pressured or in emotional distress, you have two major choices. You can take it all completely seriously; you can get lost in the drama and intensity of it all; you can feel sorry for yourself; you can allow the acidic chemistry to flood through you; you can create more distress. Or you can be more philosophical. Switch on a mental attitude that maintains a sense of humour and proportion. Bring yourself some relief and sanity.

The mind–body connection is very powerful here. An intense mind creates acidic body chemistry. The watchful witness calms the chemistry down and brings back some harmony.

The seesaw is between being unaware and being aware. Asleep or awake. Lost or found. Out of control or in control. It is as if you are a car and your mind is the driver. It is when conditions get difficult that your mind needs to be more careful and more vigilant. It is in crisis that your mind needs to be fully awake, not lost in your reaction to the moment.

This, then, is the great gift of the watchful mind – the ability not to get overwhelmed by fearful emotions and their chemistry. When you hit emotional fog or are in danger of skidding out of control, watch carefully what is happening.

To switch on this self-observation is a skill. You have *to pause and detach* yourself from the stimulation of the immediate situation. Essentially this is as easy as switching on the television or CD player, but it requires some discipline and will-power. Instead of getting submerged in the momentum of your own reaction and mood, you keep a clear head.

Yes, you may be feeling anger, impatience, jealousy, depression, fear, negativity, but if you have the motivation to pause

– even count to ten – and watch what is happening to yourself, you will immediately feel things coming back under control. To observe and manage yourself gives you substantial personal power. You create a benevolent loop between your mind and your body chemistry.

This does not mean that you should ignore the danger signs around you. Nor does it mean that you should ignore your own reactions and distress. You should be aware of them all – and through an act of wilfulness, through a clear and motivated decision, clearly choose not to be the victim and submerged in overwhelming stuff, but to be the controller of your own life and how you feel. It is a decision that is to do with your healthy survival and one that is also wise and liberating.

Your Natural Opiates

Most people are very familiar with how sex has varying degrees of pleasure. At one end of the spectrum is a small sensation of pleasure. At the other is ecstasy.

The actual physical sensation of the pleasure comes from the release of endorphins – the morphine or opium produced naturally within your body. In the first case, there is a small and localised production of endorphins, your internal opium. In the second, your whole body is flooded with them.

If you complete a piece of plumbing successfully, the sensation of pleasure accompanying your satisfaction comes from a small release of endorphins. If you close your eyes and think of anything that you really love – place, person, activity, animal, scent, colour and so on – you will notice the beginnings of an inner feeling of pleasure. This pleasurable sensation also comes from the endorphins.

Over the years I have asked many people to list their positive triggers – the things they love – and they vary immensely from person to person. Many people enjoy the scent of flowers or coffee, but the smell of the Paris Metro or the oil of a motor-racing track may trigger others' opiates. In my groups, people have sometimes giggled about what they found pleasurable and would never tell me what they were thinking of!

The point here is this. *The long-term key to a calm and safe body is to have an ongoing and healthy flow of these opiate hormones.* And the surest way to trigger their production is to enjoy yourself. This leads to the unavoidable conclusion that you must have a pleasurable life in order to feel safe.

This will of course shock stoic toughies, who think that pleasure is bad for people; that it is weakening and corrupting. But the reality is that a body soaking in endorphins provides the foundation for strength, flexibility and endurance.

Triggering these internal opiates through pleasurable thoughts or activities may also seem unrealistic or inappropriate for people who are in the middle of a severe crisis or bereavement, or in great pain. If this is your situation, I sympathise with you completely. However, I can assure you that sooner or later, the life force, the natural vitality and healing in all living things, will begin to surface – and pleasure can be guided and woven carefully back into your life.

How to Endorphinate

So, how do you get these miracle hormones flowing? Soak in pleasure! Pleasure is chemically good for you. Pleasure is the natural state for a human being. This is easy to demonstrate. Choose from the following two options. One – spend the evening doing something you enjoy. Two – poke your eyes out. Of course, you chose the first option. Just as rivers flow to the ocean, so human beings flow towards what feels good. It is a basic instinct.

The real trick to triggering endorphins and transforming your chemistry is to take small moments of pleasure and to expand them into something stronger, longer and deeper. This happens automatically to people when, for example, they are soaking in a warm bath, having a massage, eating a good meal or relaxing on the beach. There comes a magic moment when you find yourself relaxing more deeply. Something in you just gives way. A load of tension evaporates and you sink into the pleasure. It happens to many people when they are making love. Suddenly, in the pleasure of the activity, lovers pause and move more slowly, allowing the pleasure to sink to a deeper level.

In all these instances, the physical process is one in which tissue opens up and natural opiates flood through the system.

The great secret to increasing this pleasure is simply to *pause* mentally. It is the skill of watching yourself, even when you are in the middle of doing something. Here you pause while you are enjoying something and you mentally notice that it feels good. The act of acknowledging a feeling of pleasure deepens the enjoyment and allows the production of more endorphins. This is precisely what lovers do in Tantric sex. In the middle of the action, they pause and allow themselves to fully absorb and deepen the pleasure. In fact, for many, this is a path to ecstasy.

And what has this to do with feeling safe and managing change? Everything! I want you to manage your physical chemistry and feelings when you are in threatening circumstances. No more tension. No more built-up cortisol and adrenaline. No more feelings of anxiety. Just feelings of calm and strength and confidence. All of these have a foundation in your ability to manage your internal chemistry. Learn how to create the chemistry of pleasure. Learn how to melt the old frozen acid of past crises and challenges. Doing all of this will build up a reservoir of good hormones and good feelings. They will be there to support you when times get tough.

So, deepen and work with your pleasure. This is money in the bank. This is the foundation of feeling safe and good in future crises.

Every time you linger in pleasure and truly appreciate it, you do something immensely good for your health. How many times do you take enjoyable moments for granted? How many times do you walk past and ignore things that you like? A beautiful tree. A sunset. Great music. Good job, well done. Nice food. Great sex. If you would just bother to pause and appreciate the event or the thought, the whole sensation of pleasure would be greatly amplified. Do you have the discipline to let the chocolate melt in your mouth, rather than sucking and chewing?

There was a competition once in a self-development class in which everyone was given a delicious Belgian truffle. The sport was to see who could keep the chocolate longest in their mouth without it melting, being sucked or swallowed. Many people's chocolates were swallowed in a few minutes and they wanted more immediately. But two remarkable women managed to keep their truffles in their mouths for an unbelievable forty-three minutes! Believe me. I was there.

It is like the old military saying, reminding soldiers to remain human and not lose contact with the good things of life. *Don't forget to smell the flowers.* Don't just look at them. Pause and savour the scent. Enjoy them.

Sustained physical exercise can also produce endorphins. In fact, they first became well known when it was recognised that they were responsible for the euphoria that athletes experience when they have been exercising for long periods. The physical body is a biological mechanism that is made to move. Whatever emotional mood you are in, your body still needs movement – and enjoys it even if you are mentally depressed. Physical movement and other direct forms of physical pleasure – such as massage, soaking in warm water or making love – can bypass your psychological state and trigger your internal opiates, creating a biological well-being that can directly affect your mood in a very positive and beneficial way.

So, as well as pausing to smell the flowers, remember the benefits of exercise.

I want to emphasise again how important all this is. I do not want any of my readers to ignore all this advice about pleasure because they think that it is either flaky or unimportant. There are a thousand reasons you can find to not give yourself pleasure – shame, stoicism and embarrassment are just a few of them. But the straight biological and psychological reality is that the enduring chemical experience of enjoyment is the *only* foundation for feeling safe.

For those of you who may still resist the idea, I want to assert once more: *the enduring experience of safety is anchored and sustained by the chemistry of well-being*. To feel safe you must find a way to do the things you enjoy.

Using Your Positive Triggers

You might want to make lists of the things you love: people, animals, places, activities, objects, scents, colours, smells, tastes, spiritual teachers and icons. Highlight the things that will raise a smile from you even if you are in the worst of moods. It might be a grandchild, or a kitten, or a comedian.

All the things on your list are powerful triggers for you. Even when you are tired or in a crisis, it will still be possible to withdraw from the world and give a few moments thought to these things you love. Even the shortest moment of focus on what you love and the tiniest flicker of an inner smile is better than an endless tunnel of depression.

If you are sitting in a meeting that is becoming boring or unpleasant, you will be amazed at how you can control your mood if you withdraw your attention from the meeting and spend a little while thinking about things you love. It is also useful to let your gaze travel around the room until you spot something that you like. Allow yourself to enjoy the pleasure of your reaction. I was once in a long meeting held inside the boardroom of a national art gallery. The room was filled with outstanding paintings and sculpture. Anyone who got bored or irritated could just look around the space and be triggered back into a good mood.

This seemingly easy strategy of noticing what you like and allowing yourself to enjoy the sensation is often the secret of survival. Over and over again there are stories of people who endure imprisonment and kidnapping, and yet are able to maintain their sanity and psychological stability by focusing on the good things of life. There are prisoners who have experienced the whole glory of nature through watching a single ant or through observing a small sliver of blue sky. The famous Bird Man of Alcatraz was precisely someone who redeemed his incarceration through his relationship with a creature of nature.

If people in genuinely terrorising situations can manage

their core feelings through giving attention to the good things of life, then surely you – who are hardly imprisoned in a torture camp or kidnapped by a serial rapist – can do the same for yourself. People who have been kidnapped or unjustly imprisoned maintain both their sanity and their high spirits precisely by focusing on the good things and not the bad ones. If they stew in resentment, their physical and mental health literally deteriorates.

It is also hugely important that you regularly do the things that you love doing – not just think of them. A colleague once started to complain that focusing on the things she loved was not working: she could not trigger her opiates; she was too overwhelmed by her work; everything was too intense. She complained for a year. And then one evening she went back to her favourite dance class. That was enough. Just taking a couple of hours every week to do what she loved turned her around.

The Wild Strawberries

My colleagues and I sometimes call these positive triggers 'strawberries' after a famous Eastern fable. In this story, a man has fallen down a steep and terrible ravine, but is caught by a small bush. Below him is an awful drop to certain death. Clinging to the bush, he is in a state of complete terror. Then a small mouse appears and begins to nibble at the roots of the bush. Disaster is certain. The man then notices a wild strawberry growing very close to him. The mouse keeps nibbling. Smiling, as the bush gives way, the man reaches for the strawberry.

The fable ends there and its lesson is simple. Even in the most terrible circumstances, you can change your experience by giving awareness to what is beautiful. In this case, in the middle of a fatal process, the positive trigger is the wild strawberry. One moment, the man is in hell and terror. The next moment, he allows the beauty of the strawberry to alter his mental attitude. From cortisol to endorphins, his mind triggers the change in hormones.

Your *experience* of any situation is to a large degree dependent upon where you choose to focus. Give attention to what you do not like and you will create negative chemistry and feelings. Give attention to what you do like and you will create positive chemistry and feelings.

It is important to get into the habit of noticing and using the positive triggers in your life. As well as making a list of everything you love in life, it is useful to place reminders in your environment and to surround yourself with things that give you pleasure. It is, for example, perfectly acceptable to have photographs of loved ones or images of sport or landscapes in a work place. If you work on a computer, you can use a screensaver that you particularly like. Next to your bathroom mirror where you brush your teeth, you can place a postcard of some favourite place, animal or person.

I know social workers, salesmen and nurses whose car dashboards and sun visors have favourite images on them. Then, before they go in to see a difficult client, they pause for a few seconds and use the images to trigger positive and strengthening feelings. And, of course, if the encounter is difficult, they use the images to retune themselves afterwards.

Your Mind as Parent to Your Body

Some people do not take the mind–body connection seriously. They know about it. It makes sense. And they ignore it. Let me plead with you to take very seriously the ability of your mind to influence your body's chemistry.

Martial artists and Eastern medicine have always understood the precise importance of this connection. Great yogis and martial artists perfect how they manage their bodies. Watch someone walking on burning coals or skewering himself quite happily, and you will see extreme proofs of mind over physical matter.

But the greatest skill of the martial artist is to stay calm, flexible and content in the face of terrible, even fatal, danger. Yes, this is partly to do with moral strength. But you have to remember that the greatest fighters are not the grimmest. The great fighters experience no tension. Their bodies are fluid. Their minds are relaxed and playful. They find life enjoyable. So their moral strength is combined with good humour. Most people are familiar with the image of the teacher in the *Karate Kid* films; he perfectly demonstrates this balance.

In martial artists, this quality is anchored into their physical and hormonal condition. Their bodies do not produce the hormones of fear. They could not fight if they were tense and shaking. Faced with an unpleasant threat, their internal chemistry remains soaked in endorphins. They should be frightened, but they continue to experience the body chemistry of pleasure. Yes, the external circumstances are threatening, but they nevertheless manage how they feel inside themselves.

This is due partly to the philosophical attitude of martial artists. They stay watchful and connected to the good things of life. The most famous martial artists are the Shao Lin monks, men who are also very experienced in meditation and in connecting with what Buddhists sometimes call the 'bliss fields' of the universe. They try to live permanently in a state that transcends the negativity of human affairs.

They also take advantage of another powerful mind–body strategy, which deliberately uses the mind to control exactly how the body feels. The essence of this strategy is that the mind becomes a caring parent to the body.

In times of crisis, stress and danger, what your body needs more than anything is the attention of your mind. Your body is like that of any other animal, and it will respond instinctively to the danger that it perceives and senses. You know this full well from those situations when you cannot control what your body is doing. You want to stay calm and act in a dignified way, but your biology is doing something you cannot control.

In those moments, your body needs your attention. It is like a child needing reassurance from its parent. It is like a pet animal that needs stroking in order to be reassured. You will reassure your body if you turn your attention down into it and monitor how it feels.

Focus down into your body. Immediately you create a neural connection between your mind/brain and your body. A neural message is communicated, 'Hello there. I am your mind and I am giving you attention.' In the same way that an anxious child finds comfort when a parent holds its hand, so the body is comforted by the attention of the mind, its internal parent.

If you never read a page more of this book, then I would urge you to hang on to this one idea. If you are in any kind of stressful situation, turn your attention down into your own body. Withdraw your attention from external events and focus down into yourself. This will immediately inhibit the production of adrenaline and cortisol. It will block the production of those chemicals which create the feelings and sensations of tension and panic.

It is very simple and easy. You can even do it while you are doing something else. Still reading this book, a part of you can focus down and become aware of how your body feels. This is how martial artists stay so calm in fights. There is always one part of the mind that stays aware of the body and calms it.

It works particularly well if you take your focus down into the lower stomach. In fact, all martial arts exercises begin with students taking their mental focus down into the lower stomach and giving that area sustained attention. It is then useful to breathe softly and very deeply down into yourself. It also helps if you guide your chest and stomach muscles into relaxing, by allowing them to sink down. If you want to know more about all this, then I recommend that you read any book on chi gung or what is called 'internal martial arts'.

Look at the amazing self-control that this ability gives. There you are in a situation that you do not like. It could be something as ordinary as a long post office or supermarket queue or traffic jam; it could also be something as genuinely threatening as an accident or crime. Out of your conscious control, your body reacts by producing hormones of anxiety. You immediately feel the growing tension and discomfort inside you caused by the release of these hormones.

You have a choice now: you can be carried along by your involuntary reaction, or you can choose to guide and manage your experience. Instead of getting carried away by the hormones of fear, you can immediately turn your attention down into your body, giving it awareness. At once, your body begins to respond to the attention of its mind. The production of acidic hormones is stopped. You begin to feel normal again. You take a few slow, deep breaths, and allow your chest and stomach to sink. The good feeling is deepened. This is wonderful and easy self-control!

Some people may protest that this kind of self-discipline is impossible in a real crisis. It is not impossible. It is a simple choice between needlessly suffering and having some control. People who are familiar with this strategy have indeed used it in life-threatening situations. Most recently, I heard of someone who was one of the few survivors of a ferry disaster. A practitioner of yoga, he immediately and carefully brought his focus down to his own body and slowed down his breathing. He remained calm and controlled, and lived to tell the story.

The next time that you are in a traffic jam or a long queue and you begin to feel your irritability rising, press your mental pause button. Notice the unpleasant sensations in your body. Switch on a kind attitude and comfort your body with some friendly understanding. You will immediately feel the power that your mind has over your body. Your mind can override the programme for tension, irritability and fear.

This small skill that you employ in small situations of tension can be transferred to major crises. Over and over again, people with life-threatening illnesses must learn to look kindly down into their bodies. A retired medical doctor I know whose blood pressure was dangerously high and who took pills for it every day brought it down to that of a normal twenty-year-old by adopting the practice of giving kind attention down into his body. The neural messages of kindness melted the programming from decades of tension.

Remember

- *You can manage and guide your body chemistry. You can soak in the comfort of the opiate hormones instead of stewing in the old frozen battery acid of tension and anxiety.*

- *Think of and do the things that you love.*

- *Surround yourself with positive reminders.*

- *Relax and absorb pleasure.*

- *Be a kind parent to your own body. If you are in any kind of stressful situation, turn your attention kindly down into your own body. Withdraw your attention from external events and focus down into yourself.*

- *Learn to pause and calmly watch what is happening.*

4

Generosity, Chivalry and Kindness

Using care and a positive vision so that you and others feel safe

Every person alive deserves a safe environment. This is the very least that we ask of our societies and governments. But, being realistic, you may still need to lock your car doors and make sure that the windows of your home are securely bolted. It is also sensible, I am sure, to know some basic forms of self-defence.

But even if all of the above are firmly in place, you may still feel some anxiety.

You can build the strongest walls of defence and have a luxurious cocoon, but inside yourself you may still lack a basic confidence and feel psychologically uncertain. You can often see this in rich or successful people. They have everything material, but their emotional fuses are so short as to be dangerous. They are easily threatened, and quick to react with spiky words and behaviour. You see them, for example, bullying waiters and hotel staff. I know one millionaire who tortures waiters, extracting every single piece of information she can about the food on offer and then sitting in judgement on every morsel, often returning dishes and wines with a contemptuous smile. She thinks she is just being fastidious and a gourmet, but her behaviour threatens everyone and eating out with her is hell.

These 'successful' people feel threatened inside and they externalise it, dumping on to the nearest available target.

Making Others Feel Safe

If, however, you feel truly secure, then there is something about you that is pleasant, useful and inspiring to others. You are not short fused. Your safety expands to protect others. Waiters like to serve you. *The real proof that someone feels safe is that they make others feel safe, too.*

In surveys of what soldiers most admire about their officers and leaders, it is not daring courage in dangerous situations. In fact, the exploits of high-profile heroes make them feel nervous. What they really admire is the dedication of their officers to the safety of their own troops. *All in, all out.* This strong caring, not heroism, inspires and evokes the troops' loyalty and respect. Strength and courage in someone are admirable, but when they are joined with kindness and generosity, you have a magnificent human being.

This is what makes good friends, colleagues and relatives. The ones you love are those who stick by you and support you through all the different phases of your life. You will not become loyal to a boss who only shows caring and friendship when you perform well. It is how they behave when you are in trouble that really matters.

In his book on love *The Way Less Travelled*, Scott Peck gives a useful definition of love. Love is when your ego expands to include someone else. The other person is as important to you as you are to yourself. Parents and lovers know about this only too well, as do good friends, employers, leaders, managers, partners, captains and team players. Great religious leaders demonstrate this selflessness to the whole of humanity. Much of the positive power of Christianity surely derives from the example of a divine teacher who sacrificed himself for others. A good parent does this all the time.

In fact, making others feel safe is part of the job description of being a good person. In this way, others will gain the space, the encouragement and the support to do the best they can. This generosity and expansion of yourself is also very good for you. It feels great when you are genuinely kind and supportive to others. It feels good inside. It builds up moral and emotional strength. It brings self-respect and integrity. And it is also healthy for you. If you have a good and generous attitude, then the neural pathways from your brain down into your endocrine system will trigger the opiate hormones strengthening your nervous and immune systems, which again will give you a stronger foundation for dealing successfully with life's minor and major problems.

I think of two people who faced unexpected redundancy in a large computer company. One of them was a generous character, in fact sometimes considered a bit of a softy by his more macho colleagues. The other man was highly competitive and status oriented. The kind man rolled with the blow and was sympathetic to others suffering the same fate. He stayed on an even keel and adhered to his values and the attitudinal quality of his life. He tightened his belt, adjusted and soon got another job.

The competitive man became intense and angry. He was very unpleasant at home to his wife and children. His major way of adapting was to drink. Ultimately, he too got another job, but the whole process was at a cost to his family's well-being and his own emotional and long-term physical health. He had no sympathy or generosity of attitude to others.

Security and Generosity

In our glamorous and success-oriented society, this kind of supportive generosity can seem unusual and unnatural. But generosity of spirit is the most natural instinct in healthy friendships, families and groups.

People are usually astonished to learn that in small tribal societies, you can often see which is the hut of the leader or best hunter because it is the *least* luxurious. In these small communities – such as those of pygmies, aboriginals, bush-men and Innuits – leadership is maintained and dignified through generosity. He or she who gives the most is the most worthy of being leader. In fact, in many tribes people compete with each other to give the most away. The most status is given to the person who is the most generous. And the individual who collects or holds on to stuff is considered selfish and weak, a destructive element lacking the soul of a leader. This is a far cry from the smash-and-grab glamour and posing of so many of our bosses, leaders and stars.

I am not suggesting that you give everything away and go live in the forests – try that in Kensington Gardens in

London or Central Park in New York! Nor am I suggesting that you become a compulsive giver and pleaser. Nevertheless it is interesting to ponder the idea that generosity of spirit is definitely an indication of an authentic security.

Wealth and status are not sure signs of a secure person. Recent research has shown, for instance, that people who pursue financial wealth purely for personal gain are more likely to suffer nightmares and have deep-seated feelings of insecurity than those who do not. This was famously demonstrated by the tragic case of the immensely rich Howard Hughes, who ended up living in a sterile, germ-controlled white and metallic room, fearful of anyone who might pollute him.

This goes hand in hand with another sad reflection of our times: that with a few rare exceptions the richer people become, the less generous they are in their charitable donating. It is surely one of the worst problems of modern society that we have created celebrities and leaders who show no great talent except for possessing things and showing off.

List all the film and music stars you know. List the celebrities. How many of them actually donate something to their communities? This is no way to make people feel safe. This kind of hollow and noisy glamour creates false images of what is fulfilling; it generates insecurity and frustration, the cause of so much violence and competition.

Being Chivalrous

What I want you to catch here is the deep connection between the experience of feeling safe and the experience of being a supportive and generous human being. Again, you can see this in the instincts of a lion towards its cubs. There is huge strength that is put to the service of its young. It is very immediate and tangible. It is hands-on hour by hour. Successful parents swanning around in great clothes and fabulous cars do not make their children feel safe. It is a concerned and caring presence that works.

Other people can, I am sure, feel and sense the chemistry of safety. It is like a smell, a scent or an aura. In some martial arts traditions, it is well known that the greatest warrior exudes an atmosphere that makes fighting completely un-necessary. His energy and his mental attitude disarm his potential opponents. It is not so much that they feel defeated, but that they lose their aggressive motivation. They feel cared for, even loved.

This is the very heart of chivalry. The ideal knight – the chevalier – is the most virtuous of men, as well as the most courageous and skilled warrior. When he enters a village the weak feel safe. He is not a man of anger or viciousness. He is strong, daring, wise and caring. This was perhaps the great attraction of the most famous heavyweight champion in the world, Mohammed Ali. He protects the weak and defeats the bully.

Chivalry is a high ideal. It is no wonder then that chival-rous warriors were also trained in the spiritual arts. Whether Christian, Muslim, Shao Lin or Samurai, the practices are very similar. Before battle, during battle and after battle, the warrior maintains a dignified and observant stance. The Christian knight in the traditions of the Holy Grail and Knights Templar kneels before the altar for a whole night deep in prayer. The Saracen contemplates the divine garden of spiritual delights. The Shao Lin and the Samurai sit in long meditation with no response to external stimulation.

From the perspective of body chemistry, you now know

what these men are doing. They are training their minds and their hormonal systems – away from the chemistry of acidic tension towards contentment and flexibility.

Holding Yourself

Be caring and friendly towards yourself. The kind of friendship and support that you give other people needs now to be given to yourself. This is the next fundamental skill for managing and creating safety for yourself.

Although all great warriors are heroic and caring towards others, they divide into two types when it comes to managing their own needs and personalities. There are those who control themselves with an attitude of cold detachment, and there are those who do it with warmth and understanding. Both types are chivalrous to the *external* damsel in distress; they will both risk their lives to protect the weak who are being oppressed by the powerful. But only the latter – the truly kind and wise knight – is careful and caring with his own inner feelings and vulnerabilities.

And, as you know from any martial arts film, the warrior who is kind and amused about his own insecurities always defeats the harsh one. Why? Because the one who cares for himself is ultimately more flexible. The harsh fighter, no matter how tough and skilled, is stiffer and therefore slower.

You are entering here the field of emotional intelligence. It is more intelligent, health supporting and effective to be kind to yourself than to be harsh. *If your mind is friendly towards your body, your body likes the attention and responds accordingly by relaxing and going into well-being. If your mind is cold towards your body, then your body does not like it and tenses.* At a simple chemical level, internal kindness creates an opiate flow that keeps all the circulatory systems open and healthy. Internal harshness on the other hand is corrosive and coagulating; the body responds to its own judgmental and authoritarian mind with the biochemistry of acidic tension.

In the last chapter, you began to look at the fundamental importance of being able to put on your mental brakes and manage your internal chemistry. You learnt about the importance of pleasure and triggering the positive hormones. You also learnt the consequences of pausing and monitoring how you are behaving and feeling.

But your mind can do even more to manage and transform acidic chemistry and distress. *Your mind can adopt the attitude of a kind parent who fully accepts and sympathises with all the inner imperfections, pressure and distress.*

Practically, this means that when you begin to feel the physical symptoms of distress – tight stomach, tension across the chest and so on – you immediately turn your attention down towards this discomfort inside you, like a good parent scooping up a toddler who has fallen. Your attitude and thoughts towards this uncomfortable inner feeling are kind and sympathetic. Instead of wincing or scolding yourself for feeling distress – or wishing that it would just go away – you give it sympathetic attention with authentic warmth, just like a wise and good parent. You accept and cradle this part of yourself.

This method can bring immediate relief and successful management to some of your worst feelings. It works for several reasons.

First, the actual sensation of distress is caused by acidic hormones. By turning your *kind* mind down to that area, you open up a neural pathway that triggers the production of endorphins in that area. You surround the discomfort with comfort and begin to penetrate and heal it. Your opiate hormones envelope and neutralise the cortisol and adrenaline. The acid bath begins to transform.

Psychologically, this procedure also allows you to create some immediate mental distance from the distress. This immediately takes you out of any sensation of being overwhelmed. You know it's there, but you are not overpowered. Your distress is fully acknowledged, comforted and managed.

It also builds confidence. You are able to stay creatively in control of what is happening inside you, and a distressing incident can be transformed into a psychological victory.

Sometimes this process requires a lot of self-discipline and may be uncomfortable. It is not always easy to stop a flood of emotion and calm it down. It can be like stopping a train. All the brakes are on, but the train just keeps careering forward. Similarly, as the good chemicals meet the bad ones, there can be a feeling of great internal friction and discomfort. The old acid needs absorbing. This can be similar to the discomfort of holding and cradling a distressed child or friend. It is as if you yourself are absorbing the vibrations of their distress.

I have listened to many stories of how people have used this strategy to manage how they feel. One man was triggered into fury because every time he arrived home, there was some stranger's car parked across the entrance to his parking space. Another could hardly control his irritation when people said one thing and then did another. Of course, there were many mothers and fathers who were driven mad by the untidiness of their children: 'I can tell when my daughter's home. The mess begins at the front door and I can follow it around the house.' Another woman erupted with anger every time that she went away for a few days and returned to find the dishwasher, sink and draining board filled with filthy crockery. Another was intimidated by bullying colleagues.

All of these people experienced hugely uncomfortable sensations inside their bodies as they reacted to the provocation.

When they learned to pause as soon as they felt the sensation and to turn their cradling attention down towards it, they almost immediately started to feel better – after which they were more able to handle the external situation successfully. They learned to manage themselves. Even if they could not get their children to tidy up or their colleagues to behave more considerately, they nevertheless no longer went into those hellish internal feelings.

Holding Yourself in Real Danger and Abuse

To hold yourself in situations of intense abuse or danger is, of course, extremely difficult. In fact, all the strategies I suggest may seem insultingly irrelevant to someone who is enduring trauma, abuse, or great physical or psychological pain. Yes, there are a few extraordinary heroes whose self-discipline, courage and will-power can maintain a clear mind when in terrible pain and danger. Many prisoners of war in World War II, for example, managed to retain a cheerful stoicism through their terrible ordeals. But even these dignified heroes carry the consequences of a damaged internal chemistry, an enduring tension and armour. The bodies and emotions of human beings are not designed for abuse.

In shocking and abusive situations the majority of us temporarily lose our centre and barely hold on to our dignity. So, to be as realistic as possible, I do not want any reader coming away from this book thinking that if ever they were to be abused, or have been abused, they should behave with perfect dignity and calm awareness. The event may be too shocking, painful and intrusive, beyond any self-management. In these awful situations people behave as best they can. There is no golden solution to managing them. They should not happen in the first place. No one should be subject to abuse. It is not normal.

Abuse creates pain and trauma. There is damage. At the very least, there will be tension, at the worst, complete break-down. But with the passage of time, a healing process will eventually begin. Time, support and care are needed. Your story needs to be told, so that your anger and grief will fully emerge.

For people who have been serially abused or tortured, this healing process requires space and much attention. For others who have been subject to a mugging or other random violence and danger, there will of course be some level of trauma.

In the healing process following trauma, you should look to find that philosophical, hopeful and compassionate part of yourself as early as possible; and begin the process of looking with compassion and kindness at your distress, holding and parenting it. This act of self-care is profoundly reassuring, supporting and speeding up the process of recovering full health.

Most people are familiar with having behaved bravely and correctly in the middle of dangerous situations, but of feeling severely shaken afterwards. One friend of mine was con-fronted by two muggers one night. She calmed her breathing, maintained her composure and spoke to the two muggers with great kindness, wondering why they were so broke and asking about their home lives. She managed to strike a deal in which she kept her wallet and bag, but gave them the cash she had. Unhurt, she reached home, where she then broke down and sobbed, shaking and expressing her tension and fear.

In the midst of her weeping, however, she managed to begin observing herself and switched on a kind attitude. A part of her mind became a kind and watchful parent, understanding and comforting her distress. She at least understood what was happening to her and had the emotional intelligence to deal with it appropriately.

In the actual situation she behaved with dignity. Someone else might equally have become hysterical. After the event, no matter how you have behaved, the personal strategy that powerfully helps is to switch on your kind parental witness and comfort yourself.

A senior nurse once told me how she had been frightened by the bullying attitude of one of her male colleagues. She was having to investigate the behaviour of some members of his team after a complaint and he wanted to tell her firmly that he felt she should just be supportive of her fellow nurses. He asked to speak to her privately and they went into the photocopying room, where he stood in the doorway with his arms folded across his chest and firmly expressed his opinion. He did not consciously want to frighten her, but his attitude and body language scared her. Nevertheless, she held her own and communicated back her own opinion.

Afterwards, telling me about it, she wept and was ashamed of how she had been frightened. I replied that it was completely understandable and normal to be frightened. I also pointed out that she was now making a bad situation worse. On top of the original fright, her mind was laying down a harsh and judgmental attitude. She was creating a second injury with her own harsh self-criticism.

Again, do not underestimate the mind–body connection – the psychoneuroimmunological process. The nurse's harsh mind was creating more cortisol and another layer of tension. As she developed a kind attitude towards herself, the hormones of fear melted and were replaced with a more flexible and comfortable texture.

Holding Others

In the same way that you notice, accept and cradle your own discomforts, you can extend this to other people. You can open your heart, your mind and the warmth of your body to surround, support and 'hold' other people. If you are a naturally secure and generous person, this will happen anyway. Your instinctive generosity will extend itself and simply by being somewhere, you will bring a positive benefit.

This is very apparent when a secure adult looks after children. They feel safe just because that person is there. It is equally apparent in many organisations and groups. People can be flying around like chickens with their heads cut off. In walks the safe person and the whole atmosphere immediately begins to calm down.

In an ancient manual of Chinese medicine, there is a pen and ink illustration of a man, sitting cross-legged with his eyes looking down into his body. In his lower stomach there is another tiny cross-legged man. This picture is accompanied by text describing the technique of turning your focus down into your body and giving careful attention to yourself.

There is then a second illustration in which the tiny man in his stomach has expanded. He has expanded so much that he is now bigger than the man who cares for him. The text explains that if you care for yourself in this way, then your internal energy will become so secure and powerful that it will expand to protect you. It will also expand so that other people feel protected and held by it.

It is, in fact, possible deliberately to create a safe and supportive energy field when people need it. The first step is to make sure that your own body is calm and relaxed. The easiest strategy here is to just turn your focus down into your body and send it some reassuring messages. Then, staying calm, make sure you have a sympathetic and warm attitude towards your companion or the situation.

Without any effort, your attitude and energy will extend to reassure and encourage those who are with you. The keywords here are: *calm body, open heart, generous mind.*

If you want, you can also guide and sense that a warm and safe magnetism is radiating from your torso – from your hips, abdomen and chest – surrounding and holding the situation.

These strategies are very similar to those used by good therapists, teachers, coaches and counsellors. In fact, in many psychotherapy trainings, it is clearly recognised that it does not matter how clever or insightful the therapist is. What really matters is the attitude, the presence and the warmth of the therapist. If the therapist is kind, fully sympathetic and genuine with the client, that then creates a powerful and safe rapport which is the foundation for a successful healing process.

This strategy of holding an individual can also be extended to holding a group and a situation. In many tribal societies, the elders sit at meetings, watching and listening carefully, always maintaining the group. People who are good at chairing meetings also do this. They rarely talk and only when they deem it absolutely necessary. They are very comfortable and very patient exercising this invisible support.

You might want to try doing this at meetings or with your family, not having told them what you are doing. You sit there quietly, first focussing down into yourself and making sure you feel all right. You then sense the warm and safe energy of your body extending out from your hips and abdomen to support and encourage your companions. You will see some very reassuring results.

Holding the Vision

The good therapist is also supposed to have 'unconditional positive regard' for his client. This means that he recognises and appreciates the full potential of his client regardless of the present circumstances or state of distress. Again, this is like a good parent and friend who continues to see the real you despite difficult times or bad behaviour. They always stay connected to your soul. There are surely people in your life who you always hold in the highest regard and affection regardless of their troughs and troubles. It is hugely encouraging and healing to have someone who sees the best in you.

When your heart is open and your mind is generous, you hold a positive vision of your friends even when they are at their low points. It is this ability to maintain a positive vision that also marks good managers and leaders. An effective leader lets you know that he can see your true potential and that he supports you in attaining it. The success of sports captains, managers and coaches is precisely judged by how well they inspire their teams. Threats and recriminations do not achieve long-term and consistent victories.

'Holding the vision' is crucial for projects, too. A good leader does not lose his faith in the future success and fulfilment of a project. Effective leadership – in the family, in business, in politics – is the ability to hold on to your vision in the worst circumstances. You keep your eye on the long-term goal and constructively learn from failure. You do not give up an ambition just because of temporary problems and defeats. Do not give in to depression and fear. Leaders such as Winston Churchill or Nelson Mandela did not lose their visions when battles were lost or when they were imprisoned.

All of this is directly relevant to your sense of safety. Part of feeling safe is the ability to see the positive side when things are bad. It is proof that you feel secure, confident and good. It is an inner attitude and strength, which is not dependent upon external circumstances.

Having the discipline to hold this kind of positive attitude is part of the whole process of making yourself feel safe and great. And I want to stress that it does not deny or repress the difficulties and pains of life. These too are given awareness, but not from a point of overwhelmed tension. The challenges and distress are 'held' by you, with kindness, while you also maintain your awareness of vision and hope. This is a powerful recipe for genuine success and fulfilment.

Now there are some of you who, for one reason or another, have difficulty in maintaining such equanimity. Somewhere in your past, consciously or unconsciously, something happened which created your negativity. You worry too much. You may even expect the worst. It would be really good if you could turn your attention to this wounded part of yourself and give it some sympathy and acceptance – and at the same time ask it to pipe down. There is a really useful trick here. It is incredibly useful to be able to observe with kindness and understanding your own negative patterns. You can then accept, hold and *contain* them, so that they do not sabotage a more positive outlook.

Of course, this too can be difficult and may require long-term patience and clear intention, but it is worth it. You may also need some extra support from a friend or counsellor. Gradually, you need to seduce and encourage your mind and emotions away from their sadness and into a more trusting and optimistic attitude. In the first place, this requires kindness and wisdom from yourself to yourself.

In Hinduism, this approach is supported by the major form of greeting *Namaste*, which translates as 'I greet your soul'. When you see Hindis bowing to each other with their hands held in the position of prayer, they are acknowledging each other's true self. In Christianity, this is also taught in the notion that you should always look for the Christ within everyone you meet.

The Ultimate Safety – Let Yourself Be Held

There is also a spiritual dimension to all of this. When I use the word 'spiritual' I am not asking anyone to get into a box of religious beliefs. I just mean the ability to feel the grandeur, mystery and beauty of life and the universe. It is in this wider spiritual context that I believe you can find the ultimate safety.

Everyone, given the right circumstances, feels the beauty and benevolent power of the natural world. Poets, mystics, and ordinary men and women throughout the ages in all cultures on all parts of the Earth have attested to the essential benevolence of life, nature and the universe. You yourself have felt it, haven't you, on the beach, under the tree, in the arms of your beloved . . . You were in a deep calm and serenity.

I fully appreciate that this sense of deep connection and safety may not be your everyday reality. In fact, for some of you, the major part of your life may have been miserable. Nevertheless, there have been times when you have glimpsed the beauty of existence. These tiny moments need to be remembered and honoured.

It is worth pausing for a moment fully to remember what it is like for you when you feel completely relaxed and satisfied. One way of describing that great feeling is to say that in those moments you felt held by the whole benevolence of life. In those moments you felt the reassuring goodness that underlies the cosmos.

It is small wonder that religious people often describe this experience as being held by God the parent. So many prayers across the world are addressed to Father God or Mother Goddess. In other traditions this great experience is thought of as being a warm river of benevolent energy or an ocean of loving consciousness. Its benevolent power moves through you and carries you.

Some of you may go into this feeling very easily; it happens naturally, for instance, when you relax looking at something beautiful, or when you have completed something fulfilling. You just feel good and held. Or you may perhaps not be accustomed to this idea or experience. If that is the case, I just suggest that every now and again, you pause and create a quiet moment – especially when you are feeling good. Then bring into your mind the possibility that the cosmos is powerful and benevolent, and that it would be very pleasant if you allowed yourself to be held by it. Let this seed of an idea grow in you. See where it takes you.

For many people of our culture this kind of relationship with nature and the cosmos may be challenging. Tension, stoicism, pride, independence, distrust, guilt – all of these may be reluctant to 'surrender' to such a nurturing encounter. What can I say? Experiment gently with a new kind of trust. It can only do you good.

Let the benevolence of the universe and nature hold you.
At the same time, you hold your own inner distress.
Your kindness then extends to hold others and to hold the vision of hope.

Remember

- *Expand your sense of safety to include and care for others.*

- *When you feel any disturbance or distress turn your kind and understanding attention down into your body. Warmly accept and 'hold' the discomfort.*

- *With a calm body, open heart and generous mind expand your energy field to hold others.*

- *Hold the vision of a person's best self.*

- *Hold the vision of the fulfilled and successful project.*

- *Let the power and benevolence of nature and the universe hold you.*

5

The Invisible Dynamics of Safety

Managing the energies, vibrations and atmospheres that can affect you

Humans are complex beings, sensitive and sometimes easily spooked. Even the toughest men and women have their vulnerable points. Because of this, individuals and organisations have played on people's superstitions. There are many religions that have frightened and manipulated people with the threat of invisible dangers. There are also many self-serving charlatans who have sold all kinds of device to protect people from these unseen forces.

For example, I live in Glastonbury, a town famous for the number of shops that sell crystals and charms. These New Age shops are often accused of preying on people's susceptibilities. But go back a thousand years or so when Glastonbury was a centre for Christian pilgrimage and you can be certain that there were shops and stalls trading saints' bones and relics, which provided precisely the same 'protection' and promises of future good fortune. (Sometimes I wonder whether those sellers of Christian artefacts have reincarnated as these modern traders.)

Historically, the worst thing was how the state and the Church used mystic threats to control and subdue their peoples. Everyone in the West is familiar with the horrors of the Inquisition and the unpleasant religious and political politics that deprived people of their freedom and lives. Sadly, this can still be seen in fundamentalist states today.

One of the great gifts of the modern scientific culture is that it generally freed people in the West from the worst of that kind of superstition and manipulation. Neither government nor Church can easily manipulate people's beliefs in an educated society.

This liberation from superstition was useful and important, but it also threw some babies out with the bath water. Much modern science claims that everything can be explained scientifically and that there are no invisible threatening forces at all. This is wrong. There are some unseen forces – and they can and do influence you. To understand this is *not* to take us back into the dark ages of superstition. It is simply to be aware of another important dimension.

The Energies of Emotion and Thought

As modern science recognises, everything is made of energy, including you. And there are many different forms of energy. There is, for example, the energy of thought and emotion.

Every time that you feel or think something, energy goes into the feeling and thought – and that energy continues to exist. It does not just evaporate or disappear, but following the natural laws of the universe, it continues. It continues as atmospheres and vibrations, as clouds of emotion or thought. This is precisely how rooms and buildings soak up the vibrations of the people who live and work in them. People radiate their moods as energy. In fact, human beings are like electric eels. They have an electric field, which is continually radiating – not usually capable of electrocuting someone to death, but often very uncomfortable.

You will know this from how it feels to be next to someone who is very angry. You can sense and absorb their anger. People, of course, have different levels of sensitivity, but I have never met anyone who is completely insensitive.

Just as a room can hold the atmosphere of those who occupied it even after they have long gone, so there are many other places that carry an historical imprint. Many people, for example, easily sense the atmosphere in the ruins of an ancient city or on the site of a tragic battlefield.

But there is more than that, much more. Our planet is filled with the energies and influences of the six billion people who are alive on it now. It is also filled with the vibrations of all humanity's history – the atmosphere of all the thoughts and feelings of the past.

Certainly, there are atmospheres of care and love, creativity and generosity. But there are also the vibrant fields of emotion and thought concerned with money, sex and power; energy fields of cruelty, anger, greed, manipulation, fear and all the rest. You can surely imagine the intensity that has gone into all of that.

So, there is indeed an invisible environment that can affect us. One of its major features is that millions of people over thousands of years have been radiating negative thoughts and emotions into it. Their vibration and energy did not just disappear. In some form or another, it is still around. You live in the middle of it and it can sometimes influence you.

In ancient cultures, for example those of classical Greece and Rome, these powerful fields of energy were often called gods and goddesses. They were especially powerful if they were linked to natural forces. The ancients knew that people were sensitive to these forces and that it was best to know how to manage them.

There is, for example, a natural power of growth and movement in the universe that pushes aside and may destroy what gets in its way. You see it when a tree grows or a volcano explodes or a universe is created. This power can blend with the aggression of human beings and then you get: Thor! Mars! God of War! If you encounter this energy field, it can definitely influence your feelings, thoughts and behaviour. Men who do stomping war dances before going into battle are directly connecting themselves with that forceful energy field hoping to channel it through their actions into victory. You can still see the New Zealand rugby team, the All Blacks, doing their Maori war dance before a match.

There is a school of modern psychology, founded by the Swiss doctor and psychoanalyst Carl Jung, which fully recognises these gods and goddesses – 'archetypes' – and their power. Working with German patients before World War II, for example, Jung noted how German and Nordic war gods kept cropping up in their dreams. He described how these archetypes existed in what is called the 'collective unconscious' of humanity. He suggested that the whole of humanity is connected by this ocean of unconscious awareness. In this ocean of energy are all humanity's feelings and thoughts, merged with the natural forces of life and creation.

Everyone is an Empath

You may know of the female officer in the television series *Star Trek* whose main job is to sense and feel atmospheres. She is not psychic or telepathic. She is an 'empath', someone who has the power to empathise and feel what other people are feeling.

In my experience, everyone is an empath. It is part and parcel of being human. Of course, you can notice many things from being sensitive to body language and voice tone. But empathy really has an energetic foundation; you can sense what other people are radiating. Blind people often have this sensitivity well developed.

Empathy is a natural facility and it happens because when a vibration enters your magnetic field, it resonates through into your physical body, where it triggers reactions in your nerves and hormones. This is similar to the way in which migrating birds adjust their flight paths according to changes in the Earth's magnetic field; these changes trigger minute chemical reactions within the birds.

This all means that, whether you want it or not, you are set up to feel the invisible fields around you. To put it bluntly: if you are in an energy field of anger, you will sense and experience that anger. If you are in a field of fear, you will sense and experience fear. Everyone is capable of feeling and being influenced by these distressing energies.

It would be naive to ignore all this. Just understanding that there is a world of invisible energies and that they can influence your mood or even frighten you can bring some relief.

It is difficult to feel safe when you do not know what is happening around you. If you do know, at least you know what you are dealing with. It is always best to understand your enemy. It is similar to when someone has been rude to you and you do not know why. Just knowing why he behaved like that – he's rude to everyone, he is having a nervous break-down, he misunderstood you – can relieve your worry. Now that you understand what is going on, you can relax and get on with dealing with it – or even ignore it.

So recognise that you have empathic capabilities and can sense energies and atmospheres – like everyone else on this planet – and that you need to manage this aspect of yourself. Sometimes, for example, you might be in a good mood, but then feel yourself slipping into irritation and wonder why you have had the sudden mood swing. Perhaps you are not experiencing your own mood, but are feeling the mood of other people.

One friend of mine noticed, for example, that he could immediately feel what kind of atmosphere there was at a party or club. For a long time, he just thought that he was being shy or cautious in certain situations, but the reality was that he was picking up the vibrations and that they influenced his mood. Now, before he enters such places he pauses for a while in the doorway, noticing how the environment affects his mood. Since he has understood why he feels what he feels, he is obviously more socially confident.

Like Attracts Like

Understanding how energies work can also bring you some unpleasant insights that you might rather avoid. Like attracts like. If something vibrates at a particular frequency it will attract and make a connection with other objects of the same frequency. This is a basic law of physics.

It also works socially. Similar people are attracted to each other. Depressed people hang out together in the same way that cheerful people like to be together. Powerful people group together and so on. It is a common phenomenon. Each of these groups has its own energy field, vibration and radiation. People instinctively know when they fit in and harmonise – and when they do not belong.

And it works personally. You attract to yourself energies that are similar to the ones that you yourself already carry. This of course has a positive side, but it also has a down side. If, for example, you have negative moods in your make-up then negative energies can more easily connect with you. Your own negative vibration attracts and creates a landing dock for the external vibration.

Negative atmospheres have nowhere to 'stick' on a positive person; they just slide off or pass by. But they will stick to someone who carries a congruent resonance. If, for example, you are sitting on jealousy or anger that you do not admit to, you may attract to yourself jealous and angry people and energies. This will not feel good.

You might have a cheerful and positive exterior, but if you are hiding some angry or depressive emotions, they will attract similar stuff. An apparently 'positive' person is therefore also vulnerable to external negative fields. This is difficult for some people to accept, especially people who pride themselves on putting on a controlled front. You may think that you are positive and in control, but beneath the apparent composure you are easily triggered into terrible feelings by people you find difficult.

I remember a woman head teacher who was personally and professionally dedicated to caring for others and being a good role model. Unfortunately, beneath the surface she carried a repressed and unacknowledged well of anger and resentment, which surfaced whenever she was dealing with an angry or resentful parent, *even* if that parent was being controlled and diplomatic. This head teacher's professionally caring smile camouflaged her true feelings, which actually surfaced in the body language of gritted teeth and clenched fists every time she had to deal with someone similar to herself. Every time she had to deal with anyone else who carried the same emotions that she herself was repressing and keeping hidden, she could feel their aggressive vibrations, which in turn triggered her own negativity.

Once she understood the effects of energetic resonance and admitted that she did indeed carry some old emotional wounds, she began to be able to manage herself and was no longer so easily triggered.

Resonating with Mass Energies

It is best to face the fact that unless you are a complete angel, like everyone else you carry some negative stuff – and therefore you too will feel and be affected by external vibrations similar to the stuff that is already in you. You will not only be affected by the energies of individual people, but will also be touched by the collective energies created by large groups.

For example, if you go into a mood of selfishness or fear, you may connect with the mass energies of selfishness and fear. This is like turning the dial on a radio. You simply change the frequency and catch the waves of the different transmitters.

It is important to realise just how easily you may be influenced. This sometimes can, for example, affect what people desire. Men and women can become obsessed with getting a particular piece of new clothing or a car or furniture.

Teenagers must have the latest CD or trainers. In these instances, relevant to status and fashion, people are not just carried along by the usual psychological factors of wanting to maintain a certain image and identity; they are also caught up in the mass energy currents of desire. They are like pieces of wood carried on the tide and have little power to resist.

I once met an otherwise strong and wilful man who admitted to me that he regularly became obsessed with getting a certain piece of fashionable clothing. He said it was like having some invisible rodent burrowing and nagging in his brain. Nothing would be all right for him until he had it. He was caught up in a mass wave field of desire for the object. This is fashion frenzy.

Throughout the world, you can see individuals and groups of people suddenly caught up in a mass movement and behaving in ways that they never thought possible. Perhaps you remember the photographs of the Rwandan women with machetes and knives – including mothers, professionals and highly educated women – on a rampage to kill and maim members of another ethnic group. There is, of course, a mass field of energy that contains violence and aggression. In this case, these normally benevolent women were overwhelmed by the energies of the herd instinct and carried along into psychotic behaviour.

It is useful to ask whether in your life you are adding to the mass energy field of violence. There was a man who lost his temper badly in the days preceding the Tiananmen Square massacre in Beijing and felt terrible remorse afterwards. He wondered whether his own anger had tipped the global balance on that day and spilled out into the already dangerous Chinese situation. Of course, it was over-dramatic for him to think he was responsible; nevertheless he had a point.

Which frequencies are you tuned in to? Are you connected to the benevolent or the angry forces? These are important questions because you should be aware of what you are attracting to yourself. It is wise to assess how you are influenced by stuff that you do not see. You need to be realistic about the fact that your own negativity, including the moods that you hide and even deny, are attracting more of the same – and creating more of the same.

The first step in dealing with this is to be honest with yourself about your own private attitudes and feelings. *If you can maintain a kind mind as you notice and look at your negative characteristics, then the energy of your wise and compassionate thoughts will separate and protect you from the external negativity that may be attracted to you.*

Being Overwhelmed and Channelling the Energy

Sometimes people are overwhelmed by energy fields and they may temporarily lose touch with their own authentic emotions and their ability to make clear choices. You can often see this with converts to a religious or political cause. There is a passion and fanaticism about them that is more than just their own individual passion. They have been absorbed by the field and are acting as channels for it.

This passionate experience is often very enjoyable, giving insecure people a real sense of power and identity. They cannot – or do not want to – resist its force. They seem unable to do or say anything except channel whatever it is they now believe. To be this kind of unconscious puppet is, for me, demeaning of human dignity.

Financial panic is another common energy field that often overwhelms people. This may occur when an unwanted bill arrives or you read a bank statement that has an unexpected deficit. The sudden intensity of the panic may be quite extraordinary, producing such dramatic symptoms as giddiness and even fainting. Some unfortunate people live with a low-grade financial panic much of the time. I have met many people who feel shivers of fear when they see invoices landing through their letter box. I even know people who sweat or whose mouths dry up when they have to look at their bank balance.

After many years of studying this subject, I have concluded that when people go into these awful experiences of anxiety, they are in fact connecting with and experiencing the mass energy field of financial fear. This is one of the most powerful energy fields in existence and it is linked with primal fears around survival, starvation, loss of home, death of one's children and so on. Think of all the terrible feelings and thoughts that people have had over thousands of years around money and survival; think also of the corruption and prostitution around finance. I call this particular energy field 'the black hole of financial anxiety'.

This field is so pervasive that if you have a tiny flicker of personal worry about money, it is possible to connect instantaneously with the greater field of financial anxiety – and so immediately feel these distressing emotions. This is awful news, isn't it? It is a double-whammy. You experience not only your own fear – but also that created by humanity as a whole.

The group with which you are associated may also affect you because just by being part of it, you become linked to its energy field. If you have ever watched a huge flock of starlings or a shoal of fish abruptly changing direction, as if it were one single being, you may have been mystified as to how they do it. Energetically, magnetically, they are connected, and because of this they can move as one unit.

Often you can see people being carried along and moved as if in a single magnetic field – the herd instinct – at sports events, pop concerts and in stock market movements. People find it difficult or are unwilling to resist the invisible dynamics.

Occasionally these moods seem to run through a whole nation or continent. Certainly, many people experienced an energetic shock-wave after 11 September. It seemed as if the whole of the developed world was channelling trauma and fear. People were indeed reacting to the shock of the initial event, but then many millions of people began to feel an ongoing dread. They were creating a mass energy of fear, which they were then experiencing as if it too were a genuine external threat. So, they were dealing with the trauma of the original tragic event and then with the energy of the mass response.

Grief can also roll through groups, an initial tragedy causing an echoing tidal wave of emotion. This was, for example, palpable after the death of Princess Diana. The whole of Britain seemed caught in an extreme emotional mood. Of course, all the people were not simply dealing with the sadness of the young woman's demise, but were experiencing mass energies that rolled forward. But this also had a beneficial effect when the whole country again experienced a mass emotion at the time of her funeral. The cities, towns and landscape fell silent as a wave of healing calm swept through the nation.

Another positive example of this beneficial effect happens in global music events. Can anyone forget the extraordinary feeling that swept the planet as the Live Aid concert was broadcast globally? Or, before that, the incredible wave of benevolent force that swept internationally with the broadcast of the Beatles' *All You Need Is Love*?

The great spiritual festivals of all the world's religions also generate great energy fields that can be felt across the world. Many people still mourn the passing of a quiet, work-free and shopping-free Sunday, when the whole nation relaxed into a mass energy field of quiet.

In therapy, too, people may channel feelings that are not their own. Month after month, some clients carry on expressing passionate rage or anger or pain – and all this release may be of no help. I am certain that when many clients *endlessly* express intense emotions – no matter how great and terrible the original trauma – they are, in fact, channelling the mass energy field. They are conduits for the archetypal field. The sobbing or the anger cannot stop because they are endlessly acting as conduits for the stuff that is not theirs. They may even get hooked on the experience.

The woman who was abandoned by her parents and the man who was abused by his father rightfully need to tell their stories and express their anger and grief – but at a certain point they may well be channelling stuff that is not actually theirs. But, in a strange way, they like the drama and the release of it, so they keep doing it.

Coming out of Overwhelm

All this leads to the challenge of assessing whether the powerful emotions you are feeling are in fact *your* emotions or whether they belong to a greater field. My experience over many years is that there is one practical and very helpful clue to assessing whether they are yours or not. Are these emotions authentic and just yours – or do they carry a vibration and energy that is melodramatic, theatrical, even hysterical?

There is a difference between feeling and expressing authentic personal passion and channelling what belongs to a wider energy field. This difference is in the power and intensity. There is only so much rage or fear that any one person can individually carry, but if he is in contact with external energies it can go on endlessly with huge power. It is obvious that one person's anger or fear, for instance, is less powerful than that belonging to a thousand people.

What I am suggesting may sound harsh or judgmental to people who have many years experience of feeling tragic emotions. It is very challenging to meet the suggestion that some of your experience may not actually be yours and that it is time to manage and contain it. Please trust that I do not for one moment want you to repress or bottle up genuine and justifiable feelings of rage and wounding. At the same time, it is best to be realistic about the possibility of this energetic connection and to have an open mind about it. There is no point in suffering needlessly and endlessly recycling stuff that is not essentially yours.

My experience is that the difference between what is authentic and what comes from channelling external energy can be discerned at that exact moment when suddenly a note of hysteria and melodrama starts to be expressed and is difficult to stop. The first one or two times that this happens, it may genuinely be the individual's own charge, but after that I believe that hysteria is a symptom of channelling external dynamics.

I fully understand that when someone begins to express a load of emotion which they've been sitting on, this expression will contain a very powerful dynamic – and I do not want for one second to question that authenticity. But there comes a time when the hysteria or the 'drama-queening' is over the top. Authenticity becomes melodrama. At that point, I believe that the person is channelling stuff that is not his.

I had been working for quite a while with a client who had been serially abused by both her parents. It had been fully talked about and her rage had been expressed many times. In one session, she again began to talk about her parents and to express her anger. Suddenly her face reddened and her whole body tensed. Her voice changed tone and a huge intensity began to emerge from her. I asked her to pause. I asked whether she really wanted to go into expressing the trauma in that way. 'I do and I don't,' she replied. 'I'm angry for every other child who experienced that betrayal!' 'Do you want to be the conduit for their outrage?' I asked. She did not. But she did go into a career of social activism as an advocate for the poor and disenfranchised.

Instead of just feeling and communicating your own emotion, you may become a conduit for the larger field. It is that new melodramatic and intense tone which usually marks the point of moving from expressing your own authentic stuff to channelling everybody else's. You can see this easily in political and religious preachers. One moment they are just being themselves. The next, they are ranting and the whole event has become theatre. Just watch a preacher like Ian Paisley going into one of his rants. The films of Hitler addressing crowds also carry the same timbre.

At home, in a minor way, you may also find yourself doing this. One moment you are playing around with a subtle feeling of rejection or anger; the next it has become an Oscar-winning performance.

Ultimately you, and you alone, have to judge for yourself whether this is what you are doing.

Some people carry a subtle tone of melodrama all through their lives, continually expressing quiet worry or concern. They seem trapped in their attitude. They may be caught in a field of energy that is not theirs. They are acting as a conduit for the mass field of worry.

So, what is the solution?

First, you have to be aware of and understand the existence of these external fields. Just knowing they exist can bring some immediate relief as you recognise exactly why you may be overwhelmed by some emotions. When people who, for example, have financial worries first learn about the 'black hole of financial anxiety', they often lighten up. It is immediate good news for them that the hellish state they experience is not just their own.

Second, we come back to that key life skill of being able to pause. Pause. Notice what is happening within you. Begin to manage your emotional chemistry. Coming back to your centre and watching what is happening to you – mental distancing – will break the energetic connection. You will separate yourself from the external energy field because you have brought into the situation the vibration of your kind and watchful mind. Never underestimate the power of your own compassionate consciousness.

When you next begin to experience financial panic, for example, pause for a moment and say to yourself something like, 'Yes, I may be in financial difficulty – but these disgusting feelings of panic are not just mine. They belong to the greater field. They do not belong to me.' Just recognising this may well be enough to separate you from their overwhelming influence.

Imagine if fanatical religious, political and nationalist fundamentalists bothered to take a mental pause every time that they were filled with an unusually strong emotion! The herd instinct that creates so much cruelty and injustice would be disarmed. That would be a step to a more peaceful planet.

Do Not Create Negative Thoughts

There is an obvious responsibility that goes hand in hand with understanding that people create atmospheres and fields of energy. You need to be careful with the energy of your emotions and your thoughts. It radiates from you, feeds into similar fields of energy and affects other people.

Sometimes, especially in situations of crisis and threat, it is difficult not to worry and have anxious thoughts and feelings. Energetically, however, the moment that you start to do this, you begin to add more negativity to the situation. The actual act of *worrying* creates distressing atmospheres. If, for example, you have an illness, do you want your doctor to be worried and radiate worry vibrations? Worry is connected with fear, and worry energy just makes things worse. It will depress you. You want an aura of confidence and optimism.

When you look at the world and see terrible things happening, what do these situations need? They do not need vibrations of distress, pessimism, anguish and worry. Energetically that makes the situation worse. Crisis, conflict and distress need love, acceptance, warm humour, playfulness, support, empathy, compassion and creative positive solutions.

I know a sincere peacenik, desperately concerned about the state of the world, his face intense with earnest desires and thoughts of peace. But what is he actually radiating into the situation? He has his own need for the situation to be resolved because that will make him feel better. He is, in fact, radiating neediness – a need for peace. And that is just another polarity that can create more negative feeling and reaction.

Moreover, radiating negative feelings and thoughts connects you harmonically with all the other negative energies floating around. Worrying can attract the very stuff to you that you do not want! And if you worry about other people, you are directing your own pessimistic energy at them and attracting more negative stuff to them. No wonder it has been said that worrying is a way of praying for what you do not want.

Sometimes, of course, a situation may be so tragic that you are temporarily overwhelmed and disappear into depression and grief. When friends die or there is a tragedy, it is normal to be upset or to have very strong feelings. But as soon as you start to surface and regain some equilibrium, you need to think of the consequences of continuing to run depressive thoughts and negative energy. You need to guide your thoughts and energy in a more positive direction – not just for your sake, but for that of others.

All across the world, there are individuals and groups who use prayer and meditation to create thoughts and energies that are positive and benevolent. Throughout the ages, churches and temples have often centred their worship around prayerful calls for a world of peace. Particularly with the coming of the Internet, it has become possible for people to network very quickly and communicate together about how, where and when they will focus their energies.

In times of crisis, they focus on troubled regions and send peaceful and creative thoughts to them. Where there is conflict, for instance, they hold an upbeat thought of the opposing leaders greeting and hugging each other with warm and genuine friendship. They send in waves of peaceful and loving energy. In these meditations and prayers, it is important not to have judgmental thoughts about the leaders you do not like. It was very easy for people to stigmatise Saddam Hussein as an evil and negative dictator. Outside the United States, it was also easy to judge George Bush Jr as a stupid man who was in the pockets of right-wing financiers. But to have these critical thoughts just creates another polarisation and energetically adds to the negative field.

One of the positive thoughts directed at Saddam was that he was indeed a messenger of God, but sent to bring healing to all nations. At the same time, people visualised a happy and prosperous Iraq. George Bush, on the other hand, was seen as a loyal team player, a jock with his heart in the right place. His team loyalty moved away from the Republican hierarchy that had got him into the White House and across to the great team of other world leaders and all the world's people.

People who were hostile to either Saddam or Bush, of course, thought that these ideas were naive. In fact, though, these were very helpful ideas to have floating in the ethers ready to inspire these leaders. At any rate, it is important and useful to think good thoughts into troubled situations, and not to send worry and fear. This applies as much to home, relationship and work situations as it does to global crises. If your children or workplace are in crisis, keep a positive attitude. This is powerful invisible support.

Ancestors and Nations

There are also other energy fields that may powerfully influence you and these belong to the groups with which you are associated by birth. Your genetic make-up, your ancestry, your ethnicity – they all connect you with group energy fields. No matter how individualistic you may be, no matter how much you may have disengaged from your family or the culture of your people, there will still be an energetic connection.

There was a man, for example, who came from a family of many generations of militaristic and cruel snobs. His ancestors had bullied and hurt many people. In his teens he separated from his family and in many ways took a completely different direction, working as a nurse. Nevertheless he still carried the aura of his family, and sometimes people who did not know him would perceive him too as an arrogant bully. He carried the 'sins of his fathers'.

Even if you are a very good person, you may still be linked to the stuff of your family. You may still feel haunted by it. You want to be free, but there is the continuing aura of the invisible relationship. Through biology and energy you are linked to ancestral and family patterns.

You may also be part of a larger tribe, clan or group that has a particular history. This connection can emerge when there is, for example, a conflict. Over and over again, we see peace-loving people suddenly caught up in a wave of nationalism and prepared to fight and die. Their energetic connection to the nation and race, to the religion and tribe, carries them forward. If there is a history of warfare that has never been properly resolved then the energy field is like a tinder box ready to ignite at any moment. You can see this in the short fuses and sudden escalating conflicts in the Middle East and Northern Ireland, and on the Pakistan/Indian border.

If you were born a Palestinian in the Middle East, or a Protestant in Ulster, or an Untouchable in India, or a black person in a mainly white society, or a Jew anywhere, then you are vulnerable to the energy fields of conflict. Energetically there will always be an impulse to associate with your clan and protect it – understandably so.

It is so easy to understand how a young Palestinian boy in Gaza or a Protestant kid in Belfast is connected to the energetic roar of his clan's energy field. He is in a very real way naive and innocent as he gets carried by the passionate energies.

Just because you are born into a certain race, you are associated with the historical energies of that race. Those of you who are English, for example, cannot avoid your relationship with the English energies, some good and some distressing. There are the positive energy fields of justice and fair play, but there are also the fields created by a long history of war and imperialism. In this way, the sins of the fathers and mothers are indeed passed on to their sons and daughters. Just because you are of a certain colour, race, clan or gender, you are subject to these influences.

To be born a white person in Africa, the Americas, Asia or Australasia, for instance, immediately carries certain challenges. White people colonised, subjected and often terrorised the peoples of these continents. This all created certain energies. You can be someone who feels passionately about true freedom for Africans, but if you are white then simply by association you are partly guilty for past sins. You may want to shout that it has nothing to do with you, but ancestrally and energetically you are part of it and you cannot escape it. Realism and honesty are needed here.

This information may be new to you and you may not want to acknowledge it – but *only good* happens if you recognise it. Knowing about it *reduces* a sense of threat and danger.

Instead of a background hum of anxiety that you ignore, you become aware of a tension that you share with millions of others. Our poor planet is saturated with many histories of such tragedy.

More than all of that, just as a human being you are energetically connected to the whole of humanity. It is no wonder that people may wake in the morning and feel a certain dread as they sense some tragic mass events happening on the other side of the globe.

I remember one friend who was on holiday in Jamaica and having a quiet time on an isolated beach. Suddenly he was filled with a sense of tragedy and some deep, echoing anxiety. He said that he could feel 'the spirits of war swooping across the planet again'. Later, he found out that this feeling coincided with the Iraqi invasion of Kuwait, the trigger to a whole series of events that have not yet found peace.

People who are naturally very empathic and psychic may break down in cities, as they feel and sense the full range of stories that are raging in the urban environment. I have counselled many empaths who have literally broken down as they absorbed the full impact of all the energies of the modern urban environment, and I have tried to help them come back to a solid centre and build stronger boundaries.

What they all said was very similar. 'Suddenly, every cell and fibre of my body could feel every person's pain and suffering. The abused children, the raped, the ambitious, the defeated, the cruelty . . . All of it came into me.' As they regained their energetic stability, they all, without exception, said that the experience was a deep lesson in compassion.

Sometimes you might feel the group energies as you walk out of your front door. The first person you meet is rude, or nice; the traffic is calm, or frenetic – and this is an indication of how it will be for the whole day. The people are in a mass mood, for which there are many causes – weather, astrology, global politics, sports results and so on.

You may have thought that you only had to deal with your own personal problems and responsibilities. The truth is that simply because you are human you are part of various pockets of group history and responsibility. This demands a new realism and responsibility from you. Of course, it's a drag – but ignoring it will only cause you and others more grief. You and I, we are connected to each other and to everything. This is part of life's passion and paradox.

Good News

The good news is, of course, that the distressing energy fields created by humanity are only the tiniest fraction of the universe. Yes, human beings are an influential part of the Earth, but our planet is tiny compared to the vast universe. And we, of course, are tiny compared to the size of the planet and the grandeur of nature. Yes, we can temporarily destroy our environment and even wipe ourselves out, but the Earth would regenerate and come back to normal over a few thousand years.

Human beings are insignificant little creatures in the real scale of things. And the energy fields we create – no matter how distressing, cruel and overwhelming – are also minuscule compared to the vastness of space. I often call the collective energy field created by humanity 'Blobsville'.

You may be one of those people who forget nature and the universe because Blobsville is so stimulating and engrossing. You may ignore the fact that there is a reality and dimension far greater than human life, and you may not experience the goodness and vast size and power of the greater environment that surrounds you.

Are you one of these people? Have you forgotten where you really live? You do not just live in Blobsville. Remember that you are also an inhabitant of nature and the cosmos.

Instead of being negatively influenced by all the energy fields of humanity's history, you can find a much-needed balance by becoming more aware of the vast and benevolent universe in which you live. It is your birthright to experience it. You are, simply because you are alive, part of it! The only thing that may block you from feeling it is your tension or lack of attention. Feeling tense keeps you locked inside your own concerns. The stimulation of daily life may completely engross you.

So, get some balance. Weave back into your life an awareness of the benevolent environment. You can do this in any way that you choose. You know best what can bring you back to some kind of realistic centre where you are calm enough to remember how beautiful and mysterious life really is. What works for you? What supports you in this ability to pause and open your awareness to the greater realities? Certain thoughts, images, activities, hobbies, people, animals, smells, textures . . .

It is so important to stretch your awareness beyond the immediate stimulations of Blobsville. You have to do this for your health. It is impossible to feel safe, relaxed and strong if you are enclosed *only* in the world of human energies.

The National Health Service recently conducted a study into the health benefits of trees around a hospital and published a budget illustrating the cost benefit in terms of accelerated convalescence and healing if patients could see trees. Do trees work for you? If so, pause and give them some attention.

How to Connect

You have to achieve some kind of balance. You cannot carry on just being triggered and stimulated by your immediate environment and circumstances. It is absolutely necessary that you regain your connection with nature and the universe. You cannot feel secure and happy without that kinship. It is this connection that will also protect you from being influenced by the negative wave fields.

People have such different ways of connecting with the beauty and power of life that I am actually very cautious about telling anybody *how* to do it. In general, though, I have found it useful to recognise three different styles of approach in this connection:

- Contemplative

- Devotional

- Ecstatic

Contemplative people like to be quiet when they connect with the wider reality. At their own calm pace, they enjoy tuning into the beauty of life, landscape and the universe. When quiet, they are open and receptive like satellite or radar dishes, picking up what is good. When they find that which is good and meaningful for them, they absorb it in a relaxed and patient fashion.

Devotees, on the other hand, find it helpful to be passionately committed and devoted to some particular activity, belief system, book, place, object or person. They are more like laser beams. They focus quite intensely on what they love, have great loyalty towards it and feel a really beneficial response from it.

Ecstatics, however, enjoy letting their body, emotions and mind explode and move with positive energy. They often use music, dance and movement to alter their normal state of consciousness. They enjoy releasing themselves to divine madness and bliss.

Of course, most of us have elements of all three styles inside us. Nevertheless, I have found that this way of classifying the approaches leads to some profitable conclusions and suggestions about how best you might deepen your relationship with the benevolent energies.

If you enjoy being contemplative, then contemplate. Spend some regular time being quiet and appreciating the beauty of life. Walk in parks and landscape. Enjoy the sky. Listen to beautiful music. Go and spend time in the places and with activities you find beautiful. Meditate. Contemplate. Enjoy your hobbies. Relax and allow yourself to absorb the good things of life

If you are a natural devotee, then be devotional. Spend time regularly devoting yourself to those things that really touch you and open your heart. Helping and caring for other people may be a wonderful focus for you. Prayer and singing may attract you. The arts may evoke and feed your devotion.

If you are an ecstatic, do the ecstatic things that take you into the joy. Give yourself time to allow passionate and healthy emotions to flow. Dance wildly. Play with the ocean. Be with friends who also let their hair down. Whatever type of person you are, do the things that help you to be aware of and feel the whole wonderful world in which you live.

Coming back into Connection

You can recognise when you are connected back into the benevolence of life; this will be when you are not being intensely stimulated by all the stuff of life – career, money, relationships, status, family, responsibility – because somewhere within you, there will be a good feeling. The connection with the 'good things of life' will anchor in your body through changed chemistry. You will start to come out of the frozen battery acid of unexpressed adrenaline and cortisol. You will begin to 'endorphinate' and feel the opiate hormones relaxing you and creating subtle feelings of well-being.

For many people, coming back into relationship with nature and the universe – with the spiritual dimension of life – is the greatest possible fuel for true good health. Much research shows that people with religious beliefs or a sense of the wonder of life are less prone to illness and recover faster from sickness than those who do not have these attitudes. There is a benevolent magic at work here. This magic is chemical, emotional and energetic. (My book *The Endorphin Effect* explains all this fully.)

The great trick is to notice what brings you enjoyment and to pause in those moments. They are all gateways to connecting you back to the wonder of life. This sounds so simple that sometimes people do not believe it. But it is true. It is like surfing. You catch the wave and let it carry you. You catch the enjoyment and let it carry you.

The beauty, power and benevolence – the creative and good vitality of life, the energy fields of the cosmos – are always there. They do not disappear just because you are in a bad mood, frozen, frightened or simply focusing elsewhere. They are always there. They have nowhere to hide. Always there, around you, everywhere.

Your only challenge is to be aware of them. Perhaps the smell of mown grass, or the aroma of fresh coffee, attracts your attention and your senses are called to enjoyment. Pause and use the opportunity to remember the universe.

The moments, events, thoughts and experiences that work for you – you know what they are. Completing a crossword, lying in the bath, watching football. Pause and surf the enjoyment into a wider awareness. Notice how the good feeling is moving through you. Then turn your attention to all the good things in life and the powerful mystery of it all.

This simple strategy can link you with what is truly important. Do not take for granted the good things in your life. Savour them.

And then be generous with your own positive experience of life. Do not let it become a stagnant reservoir within you. Let it flow. Without bragging or glowing self-satisfaction, have good will and a generous spirit towards others. Let your presence be quietly supportive. Be a beacon of positive and encouraging stability. Give people quality time and attention. Share your good things. Stay in the flow. As the good things flow to you, absorb them and then radiate and distribute the positive benefits.

Healing War

It is from this strong foundation that you can then be fully realistic about the general human condition. The wave fields of pain, injustice, resentment, aggression and warfare that humanity has created are immense and strong. They float as large, negative influences around the planet and will channel through situations that attract them. This is why political conflict has to be handled so carefully. The politicians and diplomats are not just dealing with the individual people and nations; they are having to keep things calm so as to prevent the wave fields of fury from pouring into the situation.

Once one situation has been resolved, these wave fields of conflict float onwards waiting for another set of suitable circumstances. For many centuries they seemed to hover over Europe, causing interminable warfare which was finally resolved by the Allies' victory in 1945 and the subsequent building of the European community. No longer able to channel through Europe, an outlet was found in the Cold War between the Western and Soviet/Chinese blocs and the innumerable conflicts that emerged in developing countries. When this international conflict was put to rest with the collapse of Communism, another charged polarity emerged in the conflict between the West and fundamentalist Islam. And so history and the energetic realities continue.

The issue here is to be metaphysically realistic about the mass karma of humanity. What we have created we can undo, but it will take time and a huge focus of clarity and good will. It is because of the energetic connection that every individual action is so important.

Thoughts and prayers for peace are good and useful. Even more powerful is your ability not to polarise, but to open your heart and mind to the pain felt by all sides and the suffering that all will endure. And equally powerful is your ability to put the brake on your own anger and negativity, and with humour and goodwill transform your hostility into loving kindness. All of this transforms and redeems the mass energy fields of conflict, thus helping to create safety for everyone.

There is a classic meditation mantra that speaks all this with great clarity. It is beautifully and appropriately simple. People sit quietly and say it silently in their hearts and minds.

I breathe in negativity. I breathe out love.
I breathe in negativity. I breathe out love.
I breathe in negativity. I breathe out love.

Remember

- *Be careful with your thoughts and emotions because they create fields of energy.*

- *Be wisely aware of those energy fields which unduly influence you.*

- *Rein in any tendency to dramatise or become hysterical because you may be channelling energies other than yours.*

- *Do not worry – it attracts exactly what you do not want.*

- *Direct creative and positive thoughts into troubled situations. Visualise, meditate and pray for positive outcomes.*

- *You are connected to the energetic history of your family and ancestors, as well as to that of your national and ethnic group.*

- *Keep connecting to the benevolent energy of nature and the universe.*

- *Radiate a benevolent presence.*

- *Breathe in negativity. Breathe out love.*

6
Creating Energetic Protection

Keeping your energy field centred and strong in disturbing circumstances

From the perspective of holistic healthcare, you need a strong personal energy field, or 'aura', for vitality and health. If your energy field is vigorous and dynamic, then external vibrations bounce off you. If it is leaking, weak or easily penetrated, it has distressing effects on your body and general psychology.

You probably know exactly what this feels like. Normally, you can easily deal with that difficult relative, colleague or acquaintance. Sometimes, however, you do not want to see them because you suffer a variety of unpleasant sensations in their company: exhausted, sucked dry, penetrated, bruised, twisted tension in your chest or gut and so on. I know many mature people who have trouble maintaining a dignified centre with their ageing parents. They feel energetically attacked and drained. I think especially of one very tough businesswoman, a real powerhouse, who was limp after every visit to her mother.

This business of having your energy field penetrated by external vibrations can be very unpleasant. Often you may not understand exactly what is happening to you. It may feel as if someone has physically prodded or bruised you. You might feel anxiety when there is apparently no reason. Some people may drain you of energy and you feel exhausted by their company. You might feel that someone is stuck to you like chewing gum that you cannot shake off.

You may walk into a situation where someone else is tense, or into a bar that is filled with violent people. Almost immediately you feel those vibrations and become uncomfortable. You might also, for instance, walk into a building where all the staff are pissed off with their boss. Suddenly, you too feel nervous, and you may find yourself talking and behaving in a manner that you did not intend.

You may also find yourself being too sponge-like, absorbing what other people are feeling. It is as if the other person's emotional chemistry is inside you. Then, after terrible rows, you may feel the other person's energy attacking you, whether they are doing it consciously or not.

One woman I know went through an awful break-up with her partner who became extremely angry and vicious. For months her peace of mind was destroyed by a continual sense of having him inside her head attacking her with unpleasant thoughts. I also know a businessman who sacked a consultant who was not performing adequately. The consultant was furious and the businessman then felt the same kinds of symptoms as the woman with the angry partner; it was as if the sacked consultant was in his head demanding satisfaction and an apology.

Nearly everyone has had experiences like this. In many public courses, I have asked people to share openly the kinds of experiences they have had. There is often surprise and a huge wave of relief as people realise that they are not alone in their experiences. This chapter looks at what you can do to strengthen your field and protect yourself from those disturbances.

The Sources of Vulnerability

It is best to recognise just why your energy field may be vulnerable in the first place. There are several reasons, the first of which may simply be that you are physically weak.

External vibrations are registered first in your energy field and then in your nervous and endocrine systems. If your nerves are frayed and your internal chemistry is weak, then the external vibration will affect you far more powerfully than if you are strong and vibrant. When you are physically weak, the external vibration can just sink into you and you have no defence.

The healthier you are, the less vulnerable you are to external vibrations. If you are over-sensitive, then part of the solution must be to look after your health. Yes, another health reminder! Do healthy things. Don't get stuck in a stressful life-style. Get your body outside into fresh air and move it. Do things you enjoy. Watch your diet. Do something aerobic at least twice a weak. Stretch and maintain suppleness. Use your muscles and keep them strong. Be careful about the recreational drugs you take, including caffeine and alcohol. Watch your posture; don't slouch.

You know all of the above! So do them. You may be suffering from some kind of stress or over-sensitivity and think that the cause of your weakness is deeply psychological or energetic. Possibly, you just need some exercise. If, however, you are suffering from a chronic psychological or physical problem, just do the very best you can in terms of physical exercise – and rest assured that the energetic exercises that I describe in this chapter will work just as well for you

There is, however, a source of energetic vulnerability that is more tragic. This occurs in people who as children were never taught or allowed to have strong personal boundaries. Young girls, especially pretty ones, more than boys tend to have people poking into their field cooing at how pretty they are. I know women who are so accustomed to having people intrude that they actually expect it and think it is normal. Especially with partners and children, they have no boundaries at all and are walkovers. It is no surprise that they are exhausted and anxious.

In an ideal world, children are taught how to be confident and how to assert clear boundaries. In an ideal world the care of an infant is loving and calm. The baby emerges into subdued lighting and a warm atmosphere. The baby goes directly to a soft and nurturing breast and is held physically close for many months, receiving the warmth and security that it needs and loves. Gradually, the infant strengthens and builds confidence to be on its own. The adults around it are sensitive to its need to develop strong boundaries and applaud when the child shows some wilfulness; at the same time when necessary the child receives strong but loving guidelines.

Well, that ideal is not what most children get. They come out of the womb into the dazzling buzz of electric lights and masked, clinical strangers and into the arms of uncertain parents. Right from the beginning of your life, you were probably plugged directly into the electric frenzy and staccato rhythms of modern humanity. What chance did some of you have to develop healthy boundaries? Your aura was being penetrated from the beginning.

Worse than that, you may have had parents, siblings or close relatives who, in some way or another, were unkind or harsh to you. They perhaps did not respect your physical or emotional boundaries. They were rude, aggressive, jealous, bullying and worse. And, of course, as I mentioned above there is also the disrespect that frequently affects young girls.

A third reason for energetic vulnerability is the simple fact that you may just be naturally very sensitive. I know a man, for instance, who is physically enormous and looks like a weight-lifting champion or international rugby player, but he is sensitive to everything. He can feel the slightest tremor in the psychic atmosphere to the point of causing him severe distress.

The strategies described in this chapter will help you with all of this. Even if you do not need them now, save them for a rainy day. They may be useful to you later on and there may also be times when you will want to counsel friends about these matters.

Withdraw Your Attention

Following the strategic thread of previous chapters, the first thing that you must do when you feel yourself being uncomfortably affected by an external vibration is to turn your attention down into your body.

When something distressing comes into your energy field, the result is always the same. Somewhere in your body, hormones of fear and tension are released. The immediate first aid is to stop this chemical reaction and to look after your body. You do not want the external energy anchoring down into you, and you can prevent this instantaneously by directing your own comforting awareness down into your body.

Your first strategy, therefore, is the same as that suggested in previous chapters. Pause. Do not go into overwhelm. Notice what is happening. 'Ah,' you can say to yourself, 'the vibrations of this person or place are getting through to me.' You then turn your focus down into your own body. 'Hello, body. I'm sorry this is happening to you, but I am sending down reassuring thoughts to make you feel okay again.' Your mind's message travels down neural pathways and your body will immediately feel your own positive and reassuring attitude. The fear hormones will be blocked and replaced by well-being.

The real trick here is to notice what is happening and to not react negatively. As soon as you get lost in your reaction, you lose the ability to manage yourself. 'What? Not react?' you may respond. 'That's impossible for me! I always react to provocation.' Well, it is time to stop what may just be a habit. It is good to have other strategies. Learn to keep your cool when necessary. Manage your reaction so that your body does not chemically race off. You must stay in the driver's seat and prevent your own body from being dominated by an external event.

Nearly everyone knows what it is like to have an encounter with an officious bank manager or someone else in authority who is radiating intimidating vibrations. In your mind, you know exactly how you should be behaving, but you cannot control yourself as your body is triggered into involuntary chemical reactions. Your mouth may dry up and you communicate pathetically.

You have to come back into command of your body. Focus down into your body. Send kind thoughts. Notice how your breath moves through your nostrils. Observe the rise and fall of your chest. Experiment with some quiet and calm, deep breaths. Let your body know that you are still in charge!

In some monastic traditions, new monks are sent to spend several days and nights in graveyards. This can be particularly unpleasant in those countries where bodies are left exposed to the elements. Decaying bodies have a distressing vibration for people who are not accustomed to them. And that is exactly the point. The noviciate monks are instructed to stay quietly in those morbid situations, calming their bodies with benevolent thoughts. They do not react. They do not go into fear. Over time, they become completely accustomed to the vibrations and achieve complete calm about death and corpses. In their own way, nurses and doctors go through the same process.

It is the same in all situations of threat and disturbance. Send reassuring messages down into your body. Don't stress yourself. Endorphinate! Your body is having enough trouble dealing with the unpleasant energy that is coming in; it does not want the added problem of its mind running wild and anxious.

I counselled a man once whose sister was always rude to him and he always rose to the bait. Sooner or later, every time that they met, they rowed. I taught him how to notice her rudeness and to notice his reaction to it. He then had to keep his awareness focused down into his own body, noticing the feeling of anger and distress as he began to react. His task was to keep his attention inside himself, to *not react* and when he was stable, continue with the conversation. To his sister, it just looked as though he was very seriously considering what she had said. She had no idea what he was actually doing.

And he did not react! Not getting a response from him, she tried again. Once more, no reaction. So she gave up being rude. Thirty years of rudeness and rowing ended simply because he kept his attention focused within himself.

Strengthen Your Energy Field

Your physical health has already been emphasised, but there are also easy strategies for specifically strengthening your energy field when you feel the need. This is like putting on a raincoat or using an umbrella when it is raining. Use these techniques when necessary.

All of the following exercises work because there is a direct connection between the activities of your mind–brain, your nervous system and your energy field. Energy follows thought and your mind easily guides and moves your own energy. So, if you imagine and think that you have a strong and healthy energy field, that is the beginning of actually creating it.

The first step, then, is to recognise and think about the fact that you do have an energy field – imagine, visualise, sense and contemplate that you have an energy field. Second, you need to start thinking of it as being very strong and with a clear boundary through which nothing unpleasant enters. You can then develop this basic idea in several ways.

Create a bubble around yourself

You can sit quietly and imagine that your energy field is like a bubble around you. Sense or visualise a bubble around you. (If you are not very good at visualising, do not worry. Most people are not good at visualising. The important thing is to have a *sense* of the bubble.) It extends several feet in all directions and it has a clear boundary. Exhale slowly and imagine that your vibration is filling your energy field and surrounding your body with your own warm atmosphere. Imagine that your warm, moist breath is permeated with the essence of your vibration. As you breathe out, it completely surrounds and immerses you in your essence. Do this for several relaxed breaths. This will feel very comforting and help to exclude energies and influences that should not be there.

Strengthen your bubble

Imagine that the edge of your energy field has a very clear membrane. It is like strong transparent rubber. Make sure that this membrane fully surrounds you – over your head, up and down your back, under your feet, all around you. Imagine and sense that this membrane will only let in good vibrations and will block out unpleasant stuff. It is very flexible, so in a crowded situation it will sit next to your skin like a scuba suit.

Decorate your bubble

You can decorate the bubble's membrane, covering the surface with images that you find protective. Some people use religious symbols and spiritual icons. Others use images, patterns or colours which they sense are best for them. There are no hard and fast rules here. You can decorate it in any way that you like. Traditionally, people have worked with 'spiritual' colours such as silver, gold and violet, so you may want to experiment with these – especially breathing them into your body and then exhaling them to fill your bubble. But in my experience it is most important to use the colours and symbols that feel good, strong and comfortable for you.

Use different shapes, animals and plants

Whenever you want, you can change the shape and form of your bubble, experimenting with what feels best for you. First, see if there is an animal shape that is suitable for you. Allow your bubble to morph into an animal that you like. See what animal pops up in your mind. See if it feels comfortable and protective to be inside that animal form. Then experiment with various trees. See if there is a tree that brings you a sense of strength and protection.

There are other shapes that you may find helpful, too. You might want to experiment with turning your bubble into a long, hooded cloak with a beautiful lining, a pyramid, a shaft of powerful light or a flame. For some people these shapes can be very powerful.

Use shields

Other people find it very effective to imagine a small shield placed over a particular area of their body that feels vulnerable. Bad vibrations then bounce off it. This shield can be of any shape and carry any patterns or images that please you. It can be made of mirror in order to reflect the energy. Use whatever you feel works best for you. In an aggressive intellectual conflict, you might want to put up this shield in front of your head and brain. In an intense emotional situation, you might want to cover your solar plexus with it.

With all of these techniques, you will discover over time what works best for you. Your strengthened bubble will last in direct proportion to how much time and energy you put into making it. In general, I believe that if you put in five minutes of good focus on creating and strengthening the bubble, it will last for up to an hour.

If you know that you are going into a situation that might seriously wobble you, then it is best to build up your bubble of protection quite a while in advance. If you know you are going to a difficult family or business meeting, you could start a couple of weeks in advance, spending a few minutes every day creating your bubble and imagining yourself feeling perfectly strong and calm in the situation.

It is also possible to use shields and bubbles to protect your home, family and even your car. (My book *Psychic Protection* details a full programme for this kind of work.)

Earthing and 'Bottom'

As well as sending kind messages down into their bodies, many people find that they can recover a strong sense of energetic security through being aware of the ground and earth beneath them. Whereas our minds and imaginations are free to soar anywhere they like, our bodies are made of the same physical matter as the Earth. When we lose all sense of connection with the Earth, it can create a physical and energetic sense of instability, which then translates into a weak aura.

As mammals, as creatures of the Earth, we are supposed to feel our connection with it. This is why people who spend long periods of time working with their hands or in the garden tend to be more solid than those who do not. There is a wonderful old English word 'bottom'. When someone was described as 'having bottom', it meant that this person was stable and reliable, especially in times of change. It also meant that they stayed on their horse if it bolted. People with bottom have a connection with the Earth beneath them.

One of the quickest remedies if you feel overwhelmed or

jazzed is to get outdoors and place your head against a tree or lie on the Earth. Then, imagine that the energy overload, the buzzing electricity in your brain, is draining down into the ground. Some holistic medical traditions suggest that you should spend some time every day standing barefoot on the ground. Certainly, when people are in psychological distress or burnout, it is well known that gardening, sport and physical labour can be essential parts of coming back together.

It is also stabilising and protective to guide your body energy down to connect with the Earth's energy. A very effective and popular exercise is to imagine your energy running from the top of your head down through your body and then deep into the core of the Earth. At the same time, you sense and imagine the Earth's energy coming back up from the Earth's core into the base of your spine. I know stockbrokers who stand in the middle of frenetic trading floors and hold on to their cool by staying aware of the Earth beneath them.

Other earthing exercises include imagining that:

- You are a tree with roots.

- You are a mountain.

- You are walking down the street but under the ground.

- The fiery centre of the Earth has come up into your lower stomach.

Again, it is good to experiment and see which of these exercises, if any, seem to work for you. On long aircraft journeys you can imagine a thread of energy linking every part of your body down into the centre of the Earth. Someone I know who was very frightened of flying felt a great deal better after he began imagining his connection with the Earth before and during the flight. It was as if his body was frightened of the height and the separation from the ground, but guided by his mind to feel an energetic link with the Earth, his body felt comforted and safe again.

Loving Your 'Enemy'

There may come times when you feel as though you are in danger and being seriously threatened by someone else's energy. Many people experience this kind of phenomenon when relationships break up acrimoniously or there is bitter competition or jealousy. As I wrote above, you may, for example, have found yourself feeling as if the other person were inside your head. Or you may have felt waves of negative energy being directed at you.

You can send an opposing and balancing energy directly back to the person you believe is attacking you. Never send *negative* thoughts and energy at your 'enemy'! These will just rebound on you. Remember: like attracts like. If you put out negativity, you will attract it. In a difficult situation you must put out positive energy. You must send warmth, affection and love to your enemies.

This will, of course, be difficult if you have been genuinely hurt by someone's abuse, but you have to liberate yourself from the role of victim. The mentality of being a victim is in itself dangerous and self-destructive, because it can actually attract more abusive energy. This is terrible, isn't it – a genuine victim can actually attract more danger, because she feels like a victim. There are, however, bullies in this world, and they are attracted to people who feel vulnerable and sorry for themselves. They can almost smell it. At school I remember the poor children who felt somewhat uneasy and frightened in the playground – and it was these children who unfailingly attracted the bullying sharks.

So I am asking you to send a beam of confident and dynamic love at your enemies. Psychologically, this may seem paradoxical, even unhealthy, as you deny your true feelings. Energetically, however, you have no choice if you want to come back into a sense of effective protection. Trust me on this. Push through any justifiable feelings of defeat and resentment, and radiate some positive energy towards your 'enemy'. The positive energy will create a powerful field that pushes back at the negativity. It is only positive energy that will successfully block the negativity coming at you – and ultimately disarm your antagonist.

The most effective way to do this is over several minutes. Thinking a kind thought for a few seconds is better than nothing, but the effect will be minimal. So get yourself comfortable and relaxed. Find that wise and smiling centre within you, and recognise the wisdom of sending love and good vibrations to the other person. If you cannot find that wise centre, then just grit your teeth and get on with it! Start off doing it as if you meant it, even if it is play-acting.

A Buddhist monk first taught me this technique. Imagine that the 'enemy' is in front of you. You bow to him or her and acknowledge their soul. Then, with sincerity, you repeat over and over again the thought 'I love you! I love you! I love you!' without stopping for ten minutes. You can also use other thoughts such as 'I wish you prosperity and health', 'May your life be filled with peace and fulfilment' and so on.

For the first few seconds, your thoughts may not be genuinely positive and loving, but as you repeat the words and act as if they are completely authentic, they begin to become genuine. The trick here is to keep saying it. A momentum will build up that carries you forward.

Not only does this positive energy radiate a powerful force for good, but it also has the psychological benefit of cutting straight through any negative attitude that you yourself may carry. I knew a woman who was being bullied by her boss, a bully with an intimidating attitude and vibration. On the point of handing in her notice, she started to do the 'love your enemy' exercise.

At first, she did the exercise without much dynamism, but then she started pushing out the vibration with real power. It completely transformed her attitude and built up her confidence. Her boss could feel the change and started to back off. My friend then found the strong centre from which she could ask for the behaviour she wanted. She and her boss are now a harmonious team benefiting everyone in the office.

Asking for Help

You may also ask for help. Energetically and spiritually, help is always there. No matter how great your problem may seem, the beauty of nature and the universe is far more powerful and benevolent. There are infinite reservoirs of positive energy in the cosmos. You may feel doubtful about that, but if you would just expand your awareness beyond the stimulation and difficulties of Blobsville, you will sense the goodness and wonder of the great natural and cosmic environment in which you live.

Because its essential nature is to flow and grow, this benevolent power is always ready to move into and through any stuff that hinders growth and fulfilment. It is only tension and a closed heart – perhaps from a genuinely tragic past – that sabotages your ability to let this creative and healing process into your life and into difficult situations. So, do not block its flow through you. It is just waiting for your obstructive attitude to give way and allow its normal course.

When you ask the cosmos for help, a new psychological and energetic dynamic is created in your aura. It opens you up and sends out a vibration that will always allow in a powerful response. Asking for help is like creating a vacuum and allowing positive energy to fill you up. When things are difficult, just pause and open yourself to the good spirit of life. Ask for help aloud, or silently in your heart and mind.

You may not find it easy to ask for help. You may think you should be self-sufficient and do not want to appear weak or dependent. You may not want to admit to yourself that you could do with some assistance. I was like that myself until I met someone twenty years ago who pointed out that I was ignoring this huge available resource. She also suggested that it would take real courage on my part to admit that I needed help. I rose to her challenge and surrendered my pride. It made real sense. Asking for help and opening yourself to the positive force can only do good.

The greatest of the world's spiritual teachers – Christ, Buddha, Mohammed, Krishna, Moses – never claimed to be self-sufficient. They never pretended that their strength and wisdom were due to their own intrinsic power, but were very clear that they were servants of a much greater reality.

So, when you find yourself in one of those hellholes of a bad mood, ask for help – in whatever way works for you. Pause in the middle of the hurricane. Call in the help and benevolent forces. Recognise that you are small and that the benevolent field is universal. Invoke its aid. Come back into companionship with your greatest ally.

There are also spirits and angels who can help you. Some people have sadly lost their natural wisdom and their poetic imagination may have dried up, and they do not believe that angels exist. But I am certain from my own experience that they are indeed real. In all cultures at all times, men and women have experienced an invisible parallel universe filled with energies and beings. Trees and rivers and places and buildings have spirits. People who have died continue. The planets and the stars are powerful beings just like mountains or lakes. These magnificent and mysterious vibrations and energies are all around us.

In fact, tribal peoples, who have not been drowned in the electricity of modern life, tell us that to be ignorant of this invisible dimension is to miss half of life's reality! There have surely been moments when you felt something new and different close to you, but could not see it or name it. I challenge sceptics to spend long periods of time alone in a wilderness such as a forest; to spend the night in a museum, a cemetery or a temple, or on a mountain-top. *Then* tell me there is nothing else in the world.

Many people ask the angels for help. In moments of sadness or weakness, they know that there is support that can come to them. With an open heart and an open mind, usually sitting quietly, they simply ask for aid. And in the asking, there is an innocent expectation that there will always be a response. The response often comes as a sense of comfort. The vibration and energy of the angel will be positive, healing and supportive.

A book that I wrote on working cooperatively with angels was reviewed by the *Times Educational Supplement* with a special comment on how these 'new' strategies could be used to help in the classroom. A week later, it published a letter from a nun who had also been a teacher for many years. She said that in her educational training, all the student teachers had been taught to take quiet time in their classrooms and to call in the help of angels.

Whether you believe in spirits or not – for many people they are a step too far – you do live in a cosmos that is mainly energy and consciousness. The solid material that you can see and touch is only the most tiny fraction of all the invisible energy and fields that make up the universe. You, like everything else, are made of energy. Managing it so that you feel strong and safe is wise and sensible.

Remember

- *Eat well, and get enough sleep and exercise to keep your nervous system strong. Strengthen your energy field. Learn to control the volume on your sensitivity.*

- *Withdraw your attention from provocation and look after the discomfort in your own body.*

- *Strengthen your protective bubble and experiment with the forms – animals, trees, shields, etc. – that work best for you.*

- *Connect with the Earth for comfort and strength.*

- *Direct positive thoughts towards your 'enemies'.*

- *Ask the great flow of life, God and angels for help.*

7

The Power of Facing Reality

Revealing and taming the hidden daemons that can destroy security

The essential purpose of this book is simple. I want it to help you deal successfully with the challenges and threats of modern life. All through the book, you have been encouraged to press your mental pause button and to look with some careful attention at how you are feeling. By turning the focus of your kind mind down into the actual feelings and sensations of your body, you will be able to manage and guide your internal chemistry. You will decease the hormones of tension and amplify the hormones of flexibility and enjoyment.

That basic technique of focusing down into your own body is an effective life skill everyone should possess. I have heard of it being used in many different situations. A lad I know was once happily standing in a queue with his girlfriend waiting to get into a night club for a good dance. Some other, drunk lads turned up, shoving into people and generally intimidating folk. My young friend felt his hackles rising and his fists begin to clench. He knew that if they saw his angry eyes and tense body posture a fight would be inevitable. He knew it because he had got into scraps so many times before. This time, however, he did not react to the disturbance, but turned his attention, in a friendly way, down into the reactions in his own body. Almost immediately he calmed down. 'Chilled, I could feel the whole atmosphere in the queue calming. I put my arm in a friendly way around my girlfriend and everything was safe.'

Looking at the Broader Picture

To be fully realistic, however, the vast majority of people carry more than just their immediate challenges. To come into a place of full psychological security, to make the transformation to full strength and confident well-being, requires a deeper wisdom and courage. Like nearly everyone else on this planet, you probably carry a history of emotional wounding, which has left layers of acidic tension in your body and psychology. A lack of a sense of safety, a subliminal anxiety, sits in the memory of your cells.

You may successfully manage your current challenges, but beneath them lie older layers of distress and past fear. You are like one of those huge, hard sweets that seem to last forever, changing colour as you slowly suck away each layer. I know many strong and decent men and women who are successful and a positive influence in the world, but who nevertheless carry an ongoing sense of 'this is never good enough, I could do better, there's something wrong somewhere.' They never enjoy full satisfaction. They are carrying the ghosts of past defeat and fear.

116

And then there is another reality that has to be faced. No matter how safe and secure your lifestyle, there are still external threats. There are people who live in fantastic houses with swimming pools, tennis courts and guards in the grounds, but they have no protection against earthquakes, disease, revolution and so on. Beyond your controlled home patch there are problems and dangers, and they exist whether you like it or not.

I believe that you now need to look attentively at these more unpleasant realities – at your own wounds and at the wounds in society all around you. You cannot have them haunting you. It is only by acknowledging all this stuff that you can come into a true sense of security, because as long as you ignore it, it lingers uncomfortably in the background. If you deny its existence, you give it the power to make you nervous. The greatest of fears is the fear of the unknown. Have the courage and wisdom to look at what you do not like – and you will experience an extraordinary liberation and new sense of safety.

Does the idea of looking at your suffering and the suffering of the world sound rather earnest and depressing to you? I can understand if it does, but if you do not look at these realities, the foundation of your tranquillity and security is thin ice.

You may not want to look at the bad stuff, but as long as you ignore it, it will be lurking there waiting to bite you in the backside and sabotage your calm anytime you are negatively triggered. It is well known that angry people who deny that they are angry are often very short fused – and get very anger if it is suggested that they carry anger in their character! Equally, people who ignore the suffering in the world are often the most easily upset by it.

People repress awareness of what frightens them. The repression makes them feel safe – but this is an illusion. Before the bombing of Pearl Harbor, US intelligence had been told that Japanese aircraft were coming, but they just could not believe it. To be more exact, *unconsciously* they did not want to believe it because it was too threatening. It did not fit their idea of what should have been happening.

To take another example, in personal healthcare people know the importance of monitoring themselves for signs of cancer. Early diagnosis is a key to the cure. Not self-examining in the naive hope that if you do not see it, it does not exist, can be suicidal. I despair at the number of people who have had early warning signals of dangerous illness, but have ignored them; these people were always unconsciously frightened of the news that might come.

It is similar when observing the social and political realities in the world around you. You have to monitor what is happening to discern the signs of coming trouble. Social care is similar to personal care. Ignore a problem and it is likely to fester. Pretending problems do not exist can be fatal.

Preventative Medicine

It is not unusual to feel reluctant about looking at what you do not like, but you nevertheless just have to get on with it.

When a small child is cut and comes to its mother for help, she has no choice but to look carefully at the injury. To do this, she has to get close enough to see exactly how bad the wound is. For some people, this is not easy or pleasant. You may be disturbed by the distress of other people or dislike the sight of blood. But when it comes to first aid, your personal likes and dislikes are not important. You get on with the job in hand, reassure the child and ignore your own squeamishness. If you do not look carefully at the injury, you endanger the child and your behaviour could be described as selfish or, at worst, cowardly.

It is the same if you cut yourself. You cannot just wrap it up in a towel and hope it goes away. Sooner or later you have to look at it. Left to fester, a wound gets worse. And to be blunt, if you found it difficult to focus on the original wound, you will find it even more challenging after it has gone rotten. The person who cannot look at wounds is tragically caught in their own emotional distress. This is understandable, but you need to be more courageous.

There is another reason why people may not look at their injuries. Sometimes it is difficult to slow down and go into a watchful and caring mode. The momentum of your life may be so filled with speed and activity that the slowing down may actually be painful.

This situation can be compared to a fast train that has had its emergency brake pulled. The wheels lock but the train continues to screech forward on the track, sparks flying at the friction. This is how it may feel inside you as your own urgency and impatience have to slow down. Sometimes when people are controlling their anger and calming down, they can look as if they are about to burst until their breathing begins to come back into rhythm.

Many adults are also reluctant to look at their psychological wounds for reasons they claim are very sensible. Get on with the present and the future; don't dwell on what is best forgotten! Don't pull up the roots to see what's wrong with the plant! Focus on the positive, not the negative! Stop studying your navel. Other people's problems have nothing to do with me; it's their lives and it's their responsibilities.

But all of these sensible reasons are bluster sitting on top of frozen emotions. If you ever think those things, then perhaps you need to realise that you were never taught to be kind to yourself and to respect your natural vulnerability. Perhaps, tragically, you were brought up in a situation that contained continual threat; it is time, therefore, to reclaim a wiser and kinder way of being.

Preventative healthcare is the best medicine. It works because you acknowledge the possibility of trouble even before trouble has started to appear. But you must be open, in the first place, to looking at the issues. Focusing on what might be wrong does not create disease or attract trouble, but is healthy and intelligent.

I want you to be genuinely and deeply happy and secure, not shaken or influenced by past traumas or external circumstances you have refused to acknowledge. True hope and genuine optimism do not come from ignoring problems, but from strongly welcoming all life's realities.

In the same way that you can focus kindly on the discomfort in your body and cradle it, so you can also look at and cradle the bigger issues. This requires a new kind of courage and strength of character.

The Vicious Cycle

Having psychological wounds and a certain level of fear is normal. Show me anyone on Earth who has endured no emotional or mental wounds and I will worship their family, school and friends. These wounds are inevitable. They are part of the knock-about nature of growing up and maturing in the real world. Life and relationships are rough.

We would not have survived as a species if we experienced

no fear. As biological beings, as carriers of genes that have an imperative to survive, we have to experience fear in order to learn and be wise. No fear at all can lead to great stupidity as people ignore danger. I say all this to reassure you that there is no shame in having been frightened and having these old wounds. It is part of being human. It also gives us character.

It is also normal to ignore these old wounds. One of the instinctive survival skills in all people is to ignore what is not immediately important. Human beings simply cannot process all the different noises, movements, signals and events that arise moment by moment in their lives. People focus on what is immediately important and ignore the information that cannot be easily managed in that moment.

Walking down a busy city street or into a crowded office, for example, people focus on their destination and the relevant faces. They ignore the noise, the pollution, the conversations, the grimaces and all the other stimuli. But unconsciously they know that they are all there. This is similar to how you get on with your life, moving forward, ignoring and forgetting the traumas and distress.

But there is a cost to this 'forgetting'. An old emotional injury can still haunt you, affecting how you feel and behave many decades later. An inability to be open or intimate, selfishness, shyness, jealousy and envy are all, in one way or another, rooted in the memory of fear.

If you meet a man who reminds you of a school bully, you may begin to blush, shuffle or burble pleasing remarks; or you may freeze, feel an instinctive dislike and just walk away. When you meet someone who reminds you of the original injury, you may go instinctively into a behaviour that you hope will keep you safe.

I know too many people who go to see bank managers,

doctors, lawyers and other professionals, and the moment they see the dark suit and the tie, they are defeated. Unconsciously, all they can see are the parents and teachers who bullied them in the past. Unable to control their feelings, they slip into fear and nervousness, losing all dignity.

There is a double tragedy here. There is the original wound and then there is the sting of the ongoing uncontrollable anxiety.

How Buddhist Philosophy Can Help

Looking at the bad stuff in life, it is important to have the right attitude. If your attitude is depressed or fearful, then looking at troubles may just make you feel worse. Your attitude, therefore, needs to be filled with goodwill and compassionate philosophical detachment; this is the pathway to freedom.

There is a very helpful Buddhist teaching, which suggests that suffering is simply part of human existence. Everyone endures pain. It cannot be avoided and it is a waste of time trying to avoid it. The most important thing is your *attitude* to the pain.

There are different ways of reacting to pain and anxiety. Say, for example, you suffer an injury – a broken bone perhaps, or someone rejecting you. You have several options. You may whinge and feel victimised. You could stride forward and pretend nothing has happened. You could react aggressively. Or you might carefully acknowledge the injury, look carefully at how best to manage it and see what lessons there were in it for the future.

These reactions are completely different and only one of them, the last – looking carefully and assessing the needs and the lessons – is wise and useful. Only the last one comes from a place of inner security.

In Tibetan Buddhism, there is a wonderful artistic process that illustrates this attitude. Using beautifully coloured sand, over several weeks and sometimes months, a group of monks painstakingly creates a wonderful large painting. This mandala – I once saw one ten feet long by six feet across in London's British Museum – is as beautiful and as detailed as any oil or watercolour. Made of sand, it is very fragile and the effect is almost miraculous. It is, of course, laid flat on a table or on the ground, in a large sand tray. Many people come to admire the sand painting and be inspired by its beauty. Many also use it as a spur to prayer and meditation. People walk around it very carefully and give it the greatest respect. It is a miracle of care and fragile beauty.

Then, at a propitious time, the huge tray is slowly and ceremonially tilted, so that the sand pours out. Chanting and praying, the monks carefully destroy their exquisite work of art. The one I saw was ceremonially carried down to the River Thames and then poured into the water.

The monks remain compassionately detached throughout the whole process. The lessons are clear. Life is transitory. Everyone experiences both pain and pleasure. The challenge is to stay calm and observant throughout it all. You will not avoid the pain, but you can avoid the torture of taking your pain seriously.

In an inspiring and poignant way, these Tibetans maintained the same dignified attitude as their monasteries and holy places were destroyed by Chinese forces, and they were forced into exile.

In Buddhist monasteries – and those of other faiths – the majority of older monks and nuns carry this detached dignity and inner calm deep in their bodies. You can see it in the body language of their walk, facial expression and meditation. New nuns and monks absorb this physical and emotional balance from living alongside their older companions.

It is wonderful to see the same attitude especially in some parents. When their infants have an accident and break something, the mother stays calm and happy. She checks that the child is all right first and then clears up the mess. The child is not hit with the double wound, first of the accident and then of the scolding parent.

Wouldn't it be wonderful if all parents, bosses and teachers had this strong and centred attitude, and children and young people just absorbed it? It would be passed down from generation to generation. There's a wonderful dream – of a dignified human race.

The lesson from this Buddhist practice is to develop dignified and compassionate detachment when facing life's dangers and dramas.

The Art of Self-correction

For safety's sake it is very useful to be realistic about your weaknesses and faults. Even the proudest of lions will not attack a herd of elephants or swim with crocodiles. Pride, arrogance and the denial of problems in your character are dangerous. Of course, you have vulnerabilities. You are human. It is normal. Pretending you have no vulnerabilities does not make them disappear. Worse than that, ignoring them makes you doubly vulnerable.

The image of the great mythic hero battling *alone* against terrible and innumerable enemies was never meant to be a model for real life. If you behave like a solitary hero in real life, you will become isolated at best and be killed at worst. The solitary hero is, in fact, a metaphor for how to approach your psychological development. The figure of Hercules with his seven ordeals, for example, describes inner psychological and spiritual battles. The enemies and monsters that he defeats are actually aspects of the human personality. The monster whose head you cut off, only to have another one grow, must surely remind you of your worst moods!

It is best to follow the solitary hero's example and be courageous and determined in winning the internal war to become a wiser and better person. Formidable weapons in this internal war are self-honesty and self-correction. This is *not* an invitation to feel guilt or shame. It is an invitation to practice the intelligent and mature art of self-reflection. A major aspect of being in the driver's seat of your life is this ability to be realistic about yourself, with a touch of philosophical humour about your lot.

For certain, at some point it may be useful to give real care and therapeutic attention to your psychological challenges, but for the moment what is required is that attitude of the best martial artists. You are aware of your vulnerabilities and you have a kind and accepting attitude towards them. Do not freeze, condemn or judge yourself for any weakness, mistake or fault – and cause further tension and weakness. Stinging and disempowering self-criticism, especially in the middle of a crisis, is self-destructive. Don't go there. Guide yourself towards compassionate honesty.

I was very impressed by a woman friend who had been experiencing a great deal of discomfort and pain around her stomach. Finally she went to a medical doctor who diagnosed it as a stomach ulcer. Immediately my friend slipped into self-pity and anger: 'My life is too stressful and overwhelming.

Nobody is helping me. My children are winding me up. My finances are stretched. The whole world is against me.'

The next morning she became stressed again as she had difficulty getting her youngest daughter up and dressed for school. Standing in the kitchen, feeling her anger and anxiety, her attention was drawn down to her stomach. She could feel the acid being created and the discomfort increasing. In that moment, her whole attitude transformed. She laughed. 'I can't believe it,' she said to her husband. 'Here I am creating this acid inside me. Its me, my mind, my attitude. It has to stop!' She laughed again, and from that moment began to have a philosophical and amused attitude towards her ulcer and towards her own compulsion to get angry and intense. The ulcer healed swiftly and her life as a whole became much more enjoyable.

Great leaders, managers, colleagues, parents and teachers admit their mistakes and adjust their behaviour and attitudes accordingly. They do not charge forward, ignoring warning signs and feedback. It is the insecure and fearful manager who is aggressive when his ideas are challenged or he makes a mistake. The good manager encourages feedback from colleagues. This attitude comes from a realistic appreciation that you can never be one hundred per cent right, that you have blind spots, that you are not perfect and that it needs a team to have all-round vision. Being realistic about yourself is a sign of depth and maturity.

Moreover, it is no good smiling at critical feedback if deep down you really want to kill the bearer of the message. The effective leader maintains an *authentic* warmth and genuinely appreciates the insights of those who put forward new and challenging ideas. This can only come from a foundation of psychological security, which you can develop through the skills of pausing and managing your internal chemistry. This brings you back to pausing and cradling any aspect of yourself that is in distress. From this centre of self-management, you can extend yourself generously to others. But you cannot do this if you are busy defending your pride from a place of emotional insecurity.

If you have never previously been honest about your faults or treated them with kindness, then approach them one small step at a time. Pause and focus on a small weakness. Remembering the wonder and beauty of life, connecting with the world beyond Blobsville, with a kind attitude sending friendly endorphinating signals down into your body, observe your weakness with an attitude of friendship and acceptance. Then give yourself full marks and high praise for a new and courageous act.

Group Blindness

Groups, as much as individuals, have trouble looking at their own weaknesses and blind spots. It is as if people in groups make an unconscious pact to ignore the truth and support each other's illusions.

For at least twenty years before the tragic attacks of 11 September 2001, for example, professors of international politics and conflict had been consistently pointing out that the future of armed struggle and war would include significant terrorism. There were many discussions about what this might look like, including smuggling nuclear devices into the centres of cities, the use of biological weapons and aircraft hijackings. It was clearly recognised that the usual national defences could be easily penetrated.

In analysing the possible causes of such attacks, it was well recognised that enduring injustices in the global economic and political system were producing large groups of resentful people, who were turning to religious and nationalist fundamentalism in order to find some psychological solace and power.

This kind of information was well known but continually ignored. Even after 11 September many people were still blithely ignoring it, preferring to caricature the terrorists as dumb, jealous and evil enemies – with no regard for the historical context. To ignore the historical and political causes is psychologically weak behaviour. It lacks wisdom. It stores up more trouble for the future.

It is obvious, isn't it? If part of the world is rich and the other part is filled with hunger and poverty, there is bound to be anger. What else do you expect of young men whose pride is daily rubbed in the dirt? Killing them is one answer. Planning for the future is another.

A true sense of security, therefore, involves looking openly not only at your own wounds, but also at those in the community around you. There are genuine threats there and they require careful awareness. Ignoring them is to create a dangerous future.

This then requires that you do not get caught up in the mass mood of a group, but that you maintain your independent centre. When necessary, it also requires that you have the courage to represent truth and honesty when others would prefer to be carried along by an emotional and prejudiced dynamic.

Be Realistic

It is absolutely necessary, therefore, to be realistic about the world. From an inner centre of kind and philosophical observation; from a foundation of holding and guiding your internal chemistry; from an appreciation that nature and the universe are far greater than any human tragedy; from strength and courage – from these basic attitudes, you will find it both easy and reassuring to look honestly at the realities.

At a certain point you have to mature and wise up. From this stance, you can love everyone and also recognise the tragic truth that almost everyone – given the worst circumstances – is capable of abusive and treacherous behaviour. To deny that all people can be both angels and demons is to deny the essential paradox and passion of being human.

This is a very tricky area for some people. There is only so much reality you may be able to take. Reading the newspaper or watching television, how do you react when you see images of starvation and cruelty in front of you? Do you quickly turn the page? Switch channels? Or are you able to look at what is happening in your world?

The world can indeed be dangerous. This is not unreasonable information. Nor is it meant to frighten. It is definitely not a hopeless observation. It is just the way that life is, here on this planet. Human beings can be lovingly benevolent and they can be sadistic. You can create heaven and you can create hell.

To be truly free of fear is to be able to look at all this pain and threat – and stay strong and positive. This is not easy, but it is morally powerful and is the mark of a great human being. I fully recognise, however, that there are some people who are genuinely vulnerable when faced with these realities. If you are one of these people, continue to be careful with yourself and do not put your emotions at risk.

Roar Like a Lion

Looking at your problems and those of the world requires courage and wilfulness. There is a moral strength that is needed here. To turn your eyes to look at something dangerous, ugly or unpleasant requires wilful energy. There come times when you have to break through your resistance and do what is right.

So much of this book has been focused on developing wise kindness within yourself, but this truly has to be balanced with an attitude that is more forceful. The lion and the lion's cubs feel safe because they have the instinct and the will, when necessary, to attack and be aggressive.

Within yourself – within the great campaign for your own personal growth – you must have some of this heroic courage if you are to manage your own inner daemons. There must be forceful action. You must be able, when needed, to assert your will and to push through resistance. This is *creative* aggression. It is good for your growth and it is also good for others. The woman who finally laughed at her attitude and her ulcer was demonstrating courage and creative aggression.

Yes – from a spiritual perspective – there is universal love and healing, but there is also an explosive force of creation that runs through nature and the universe. Let some of this force flow through you when needed. It is the source of birth, growth and development.

If you have ever experienced or witnessed childbirth, you will know that this most sacred and delicate of times is in fact filled with the fury of creation. The emergence of the infant is indeed hard labour, creative aggression.

I suppose that the essence of this power comes from the origins of our cosmos. Big Bang. Big Breath. However it happened, an incomprehensible power was released and is still echoing and vibrating through everything. The continual birth of new life is immediate testimony to this reality. New life emerges with force. This may happen slowly, as with the growth of a tree from seed or the development of a baby into child and then adult. It may happen suddenly, like a volcanic eruption or the birth of a galaxy.

In human beings, this force demonstrates itself in a will to survive. Pause right now, shut your mouth and use your fingers to close your nostrils. How long can you stay relaxed without breathing? At a certain point, an instinctive force will surge up within you to breathe again! You will live!

Just as a tree may push aside whatever is in the way of its growth, so too will you. Often I watch people who consider themselves to be weak victims of the world, always complaining, always feeling victimised – but they sure do survive! Their moaning grinds down other people like relentless waves against a cliff, but they have not curled up into a ball behind the fridge and died. Even in their complaining, there is a consistency that goes on and on. They are survivors.

There is an instinctive life force that drives people to continue. People *will* continue to breathe. People *will* get the food they need. Just because you are alive, you have this force within you. Let its fire burn.

Develop Your Creative Aggression

Many people today are familiar with the idea that there must be balance in the universe and with the Eastern concepts of Yin and Yang. Yin is soft, yielding and holds things together. Yang is firm, expanding and expressive. Especially within human beings, these two need to be in balance. Both the totally receptive wimp and the powerful obsessive leader are boring and out of balance.

In many of the strategies in this book, such as pausing and giving caring attention down into your body, you have been working with a Yin approach – soft, yielding and holding together. In the centre of this method, however, your mind and intention have needed to be clear and disciplined. This is Yang. To do the mental and attitudinal focusing you need to develop moral strength and to assert your will.

This strength and this creative aggression must also be expressed outwards into the world. As you know, we are all intimately interconnected. This connection comes from many sources, including ecology, politics, genes and our shared fields of energy. Our wounded world surely demands that we show some creative force, that we counter abuse and that we build things that are good.

It is important, therefore, to learn how to manage and express your power wisely. This is one of the necessary tools of security. It is very basic and some people do it naturally. Others, as we tragically know, express too much force.

If you have never been good at creating boundaries and saying 'no', then be honest with yourself about this. I strongly recommend that you spend three months learning a hard martial art – karate, aikido, kick-boxing, street self-defence and so on. If you have children, I absolutely recommend that they learn some of these disciplines and that you encourage their natural boundaries. Infants and toddlers are capable of expressing clear 'no's, and these should be respected and wisely encouraged.

If you have never been good at giving criticism or receiving it, if you find arguments difficult and intimidating, I also strongly recommend that you look carefully into what is called 'assertiveness training', which will teach you how to communicate strongly without being abusive.

It is everyone's right – just because they are alive – to have their own space and to feel safe within it. There may come times when you have to powerfully assert and defend that right both for yourself and for others.

There is a natural and healthy fury, force and fire, that runs through nature and the cosmos. Tend this fire within yourself and, when appropriate, let it flame to your benefit and to that of those around you.

Remember

- *Look clearly at your psychological history so that it does not haunt you.*

- *Be watchful and kind towards yourself. Old wounds must not be allowed to fester.*

- *Develop philosophical compassion.*

- *Look maturely at the problems and suffering in the world.*

- *Be realistic about the dangers of life, but never lose sight of the bigger picture.*

- *Your caring side must be balanced with creative aggression. Fight for what you believe in.*

- *If needed, get some training in the hard martial arts and assertiveness.*

- *Allow the fire and fury of nature and the universe to flame and express themselves through you.*

8
A Safe and Great Soul

Moving on from safety to fulfilment

The world has changed. In a matter of hours you can physically be anywhere. Electronically you can be everywhere. Through global economics, you are connected to everyone on the planet. Through mass media, the tragedies and celebrations of all humanity are in your living room and even in your pocket. You are now a global citizen and, through the complex web of interdependence, you are linked to everything. What you do matters. And what other people do matters to you. We all affect each other.

Being a Global Citizen

Being a global citizen, a participant in this global village, is very different from belonging to some isolated hunter-gatherer tribe deep in the Amazon rainforest or the African savannah. Here in the 21st century we can know about every-one. Who is a true stranger? But in small tribes, the people may only know of their own people – all one or two hundred of them, or even less. Strangers are creatures from another world. Many tribal peoples are very wary and hostile to strangers. They do not trust them. They may even eat them.

They may even eat other people! But inside the tribe, these people are incredibly kind, caring and generous to each other. Anthropologists have described many tribes – such as the Kalahari bushmen, Australian aboriginals and Eskimo Innuits – in which the members share absolutely everything and all goods are held in common ownership. Children and the vulnerable are treated with the utmost love and respect. There is little conflict and no bullying.

But when these people encounter strangers or another tribe, they may become cautious in the extreme and not even recognise the strangers as fellow humans. In fact, in some tribal languages, strangers are called 'those who do not exist' or the 'non-humans'. These 'others' are the ones who can be eaten. Yet, within their own small communities, there is great peace and benevolence.

If you have children or have really loved someone, you will probably have had a similar experience. You would lay down your life for your beloved. What greater act of love and self-lessness? And you would also probably kill for your children and beloved if they needed food or protection. What a paradox. Self-sacrificing and generous at home, yet a killer of those beyond the family. In many situations this seems to be a basic instinct. In one way or another it can be seen every-where in the modern world: in street gangs, sports clubs, ladettes and so on.

In small tribes the instinct of sharing with your kin is also supported by the fact that you cannot hide your behaviour; you cannot cheat. Everything is seen. Actions or attitudes that may be selfish are quickly reined in. The tribe cannot afford to have an egoistic bully or horder of food in its midst; it destroys the social cohesion and can actually be dangerous in times of famine or natural crisis.

In the modern world, through travel, economics and media, we are also now neighbours to everyone. There is a global village, and there are no more tribes of strangers. There are six billion people in our community. We are one huge tribe. But in our huge community, the social glue that effectively ensures that people are generous and well-behaved with each other does not exist. You can be invisible, unaccountable and irresponsible, living your life unseen. There is no cohesive social force making sure you observe the tribal spirit.

Yes, there are laws and police forces in our modern countries, and there is a general sense of what is right and wrong, but the behaviour of millions of people is selfish, greedy and harmful. We have lost the safety of the tribal village.

How then are you to behave? Are all these people in the global village your family or your enemies? Share everything or eat them? One choice is to join or create small tribes in which you feel safe: they will include elements that you identify with, such as your clique, religion, nationality, gender, sexual inclination, status group and so on. The challenge here is to avoid the emotional immaturity and cruelty of group elitism, religious fundamentalism and jingoistic nationalism, all of which are violent to outsiders. However, we need to appreciate that in a world of uncertainty, where people have no clear status or identity, where their psychological life is insecure, the certainty of extremism is alluring and may seem the only clear path. It is no wonder that young people cut off from the education, prosperity and life chances enjoyed by those with a secure and economically stable household should find their way into gangs. Here they can find the emotional security of a clear identity and significant status.

Many millions of people, of course, choose to join that enormous global family: the planetary middle class with its dream and reality of nice homes, good cars and decent holidays. This is a huge clan, but unfortunately it often behaves like most other clans, protecting and respecting those within it, but ignoring or hurting people who are not the same. The poor do not belong to it. The poor are outsiders and even if they are not eaten, their lives can be savaged by the consumer demands of the global middle class. The eating habits of those of us in the developed world – for example our desire for fresh and varied imported produce – can destroy local economies and agriculture, transforming self-sustaining tribal peoples into impoverished and starving folk. We eat. They starve. It is the same old story. In-group. Out-group.

There are important decisions to be made here. In this new world, there are new moral demands. You can of course just ignore the moral questions, join in the mayhem of the rat race, get your snout in the trough and survive as best you can. Or you can choose a path of balance, strength and generosity. You can choose to make the world more secure for everyone.

You need physical and psychological safety – this is the foundation for healthy personal growth – but you cannot achieve this in a world where other people feel insecure. They will bear grudges. They may want to eat you. All across Africa, Asia and south America, marginalised and hungry people have risen with a vengeance and will naturally continue to do so – wouldn't you if your children were starving? – and the middle classes have been surprised.

If, therefore, you yourself want to feel both safe and great – if you want your family and friends to feel safe – then you have no choice but to engage with the wider issues. This is partly self-interest, but it is also a powerful moral call.

This is the path of an adult; you can no longer depend on the parents and the tribal elders for guidance. You are not living in an open village, your life visible to everyone in the clan and, therefore, are not being steered into maintaining your civil responsibilities. In the modern world, the elder who guides you is the inspiration and integrity of your own soul.

For certain, like everyone, you need a sense of belonging. Why not belong to the great tribe of the good and safe people? Why not look beyond the immediate communities to which you belong and begin to take responsibility for the whole community of life? This does not mean that you have to join the protesters against globalisation or take a year off to work with people in the developing world (though you could), but it certainly means that you can begin to open your awareness to the people you have previously ignored or even disliked.

The world desperately needs an end to the spirals of conflict that kill, hurt and starve so many. This surely begins in your heart and mind. Among people of all political persuasions and all levels of society, there are always those whose awareness expands beyond their own small group. When a political leader or a sports person speaks well of an opponent, it is like a breath of fresh air. When a powerful organisation, such as a petroleum company, begins to openly and authentically look at the effect it has on poorer communities and the environment, you can tangibly feel a wave of encouragement and reassurance. When an Israeli Jew understands the viewpoint of a Palestinian and vice versa, when a white person extends his focus to empathise with a black person, when a man seeks to understand the position of women, when adults truly understand children – then some deep and healing magic is happening for everyone.

I have on my desk as I write a photograph of an orthodox Jew, a devout Muslim and a Buddhist monk praying for peace together on a hill in Jerusalem. Behind them, you can see the golden dome of the great Mosque that stands close to the wailing wall of Solomon's Temple. How wonderful that representatives of the two warring sides should be openly praying together to bring healing to their land. And how perfect that they have been joined by a Buddhist monk who is wandering the world and seeking to bring peace to troubled communities. I was told that people who experienced their prayer work were deeply moved by it. Normally cynical Israelis and Palestinians softened and smiled as they came close to the aura of this prayer group. And once, when there was rioting, the police cleared everyone from the area except the prayer group. 'You can stay,' the police said. 'We know that you are doing good.'

This kind of dramatic action can be replicated by you every time that you open your heart and mind to someone you previously considered an enemy. It is no use staying trapped in a world of stereotypes. Capitalists are bad. Communists are bad. Terrorists, fundamentalists, Westerners . . . everyone can be stereotyped and you can easily go into a critical polarity, judging and disliking. With every critical judgement you feed the mass energy field of prejudice and conflict. Every time you have the courage and purposefulness to cut through your own prejudice, you send a ripple of liberation through the energy fields of conflict. Every time that you melt an intolerance or bigotry, you heal part of the greater energy field of prejudice.

Growing to Excellence

Perhaps you did not expect this call to become an engaged and responsible citizen of this beautiful planet – to create safety for everyone. But why else become safe and great yourself? Surely not just to enjoy your own comfort, smugly ignoring everything else.

There is a drive in all life to grow, transform and fulfil. This drive is in human beings, too. Often, however, it becomes translated into achieving material success and power. But this desire for status is just camouflage over what really matters to people. What people really want is to become fully themselves, to grow and reach their full potential. This is not judged by the labels you wear, the beauty and value of your home or the size of your bank account.

Your fulfilment is known by how happy and at peace you are within yourself, and by your integrity in relation to the whole community of life. Your fulfilment is to do with wisdom and generosity, strength, creativity and caring. It is to do with how you feel inside and how this is of use to those around you.

So many times, I meet rich and successful people who are hollow. And so many times, I meet down-to-earth good people who are solid and have a contentment denied to those who are still looking for the mistaken kind of material fulfilment.

Surely, just as a seed grows to flower, so a human grows to

wisdom and generosity. You may have reason to be cynical about this, but given secure circumstances where people are loved, nourished and do not live in fear, they naturally flow into creative and positive growth.

If you follow a path that is completely lost in the illusions of success and materialism, you are essentially out of harmony with this drive to fulfilment, this greater flow of life. Out of synch with the flow, you will know deep down that something is wrong and this in itself will create anxiety – the insecurity and fear that come from being cut off from the heart of life, disconnected, and not belonging, with no secure foundation for your sense of self.

This is why so many people become more sad and neurotic when they achieve material success. They had thought that fulfilling those goals would be satisfying, that it would make them feel full and good. But material success does not deliver that kind of deep satisfaction and integrity. Thus, their most basic desires have been thwarted. In success, they are tragically defeated. Their genuine needs have, in fact, been teased to the point of torture. Surrounded by expensive cars and homes, they still anaesthetise their distress with drugs, alcohol and other compulsions. They have little peace.

To feel safe, to feel integrity and connection, there is no choice ultimately but to focus on your moral and spiritual development. This is not a call for you to climb into a religious or spiritual box of beliefs – though for some, religion works well. It is not a call for you to become some earnest and puritanical do-gooder. It is only to remind you again of your true place in the cosmos and the responsibilities that go with it. Enjoy the fabulous creativity, mystery and beauty of life – and care for others.

Encouraging Your Soul

Again, how are you to behave in the modern world?

I believe that you must make clear decisions and choices. For your own development and for the sake of others, you cannot afford to drift. The 'drifting' I am talking about here is to do with morality, caring and courage. It is to do with being a strong human being and not just a survivor.

People can get so easily caught up in the drama and urgency of their careers and their emotional needs. Work can become overwhelming and consuming. Relationships can be all about only getting what you need. The English philosopher Bertrand Russell once wrote, 'One of the symptoms of approaching a nervous breakdown is the belief that one's work is terribly important.' For 'work' you could substitute relationships, looks, status and so on.

Nobody has ever said that it easy being human. To steer a moral course, to be generous in your life, requires motivation and a clear choice. You have to decide that is how you want to be. No one is going to wave a magic wand over you so that suddenly you will be transformed into a better person. It is a decision that you will make because that is where you will find integrity and self-respect.

Making the decision to steer your life more wisely may seem simple, but to see it through takes real determination and encouragement. Like a New Year's resolution to lose weight or stop smoking, the idea is easy but the accomplishment is difficult. If you are lucky there will be good friends to encourage you, but ultimately the real encouragement must come from yourself, from your core, from your own soul.

To many people the idea of your soul or spirit may seem

mysterious and intangible, but I believe that it is very direct and simple. There is a powerful life force at your core, which is who you really are.

I wish that I could help better and be more clear about how to heighten your awareness of this spirit within you, but the longer I study and teach in this field, the more I realise and celebrate that every person has their own path, their own way. This is hardly surprising because the relationship between you and your soul is unique. No wonder that so many religious poems talk about it as a mysterious love affair, as a seduction, as a gradual meeting, embrace and then ecstasy.

You experience your soul at different times. There are times perhaps when you have a flowing and generous heart, and when your mind is bright and kind – that is you being your soul. There are times when you may pause, calm and feel a deep peace, and that surely is your soul. Sometimes you may be working with a clear determination and sense of being in the right place at the right time – this too is an expression of your soul.

And there are times when you can see and feel only too easily the suffering in the world. In reaction, you do not disappear into dark depression, but a source of love wells up within you to witness these tragedies of life with poignancy and compassion. This awful feeling of love and pain, of beauty and tragedy, is the source of great art, the poetry of the human condition. It is also your soul.

Sometimes your spirit also calls you, even demands, that you take action to relieve the injustice, poverty and pain in the world. And there are times when a voice within you roars or insistently summons you to change your life. That too is the call of your soul.

Then there are the dreams and experiences during the

course of which you feel that you meet a wonderful but invisible presence. Often people interpret this as meeting God or some angelic being, but this too can be your soul.

A man once recounted to me a magnificent dream in which he had met this majestic presence who filled him with a sense of strength, confidence and healing. He was still glowing from the experience when he told me about it. 'Who was he?' he asked. 'Was he your soul?' I asked. The man was filled immediately with a sense of unworthiness and inability to imagine that he could be so wonderful. But there was a huge ring of truth to this interpretation and, as he sat quietly, his undue humility melted away as he accepted and considered the implications.

You are surely very familiar with one or more of the above experiences. You have probably never paused to consider their significance. They are evidence that there is something deep and good and wise within you. It is good to pause and contemplate this deeper aspect of yourself, your core.

Do you have a conscious relationship with this part of yourself? Do you honour and recognise your core? Do you listen to your soul, your conscience, your creative spirit? I do not need to explain to you how to do this. I encourage you, though, to take this aspect of yourself very seriously indeed. Be aware of it. Remember it.

To be in a relationship with your soul is to be called to a wiser, more loving and more creative life.

Three Crucial Ingredients

I believe there are three crucial daily practices, which need to be in your life if you are to create an authentic and enduring foundation for feeling safe.

- The first is *self-reflection*.

- The second is *connecting with the good things*.

- The third is *doing good*.

They need, I suggest, to be anchored into and become part of your everyday life. They will provide you with a strong focus to counterbalance the stimulation, demands, addictions, tension and negativity of your daily life.

Self-reflection

It is difficult to manage your health, your relationships and your development successfully if you do not give yourself some careful time and focus. This means that on a daily basis you need to take some private minutes to monitor and assess how you are doing. Some people can do this with a note pad and the television on in the background. Others do it in a calm, meditative way. Keeping a daily journal is also good.

In these self-reflective moments, it is useful to track back over the previous hours and look at how you behaved and felt. Remember that the stuff you would rather forget is never forgotten, but lingers on unconsciously.

There are regular questions that you can put to yourself. How is your body feeling? Where is there discomfort? Are you giving it kind and wise attention? What is the source and meaning of this discomfort? Have you behaved badly or lost control of your feelings in the previous hours? Notice these events. Be honest with yourself.

This time of self-reflection brings the awareness and the light of your wise and kind mind to parts of yourself that would rather hide, haunt and influence you from the dark. It is by far the best strategy to look clearly at your internal shadows.

Notice also the good and successful things you have done. Did you cook a good meal? Did you start that task? Did you reach out to that person?

I hope that by this stage in this short book, you will know that you must not do self-reflection with an attitude that is depressed or judgmental. Looking at your shadows from a begrudging or victimised perspective will only make things worse. So if you are feeling really bad and cannot raise the slightest hint of a philosophical smile, then do not do it.

Pausing and auditing how you are doing needs to be done in a way that is philosophically kind. Self-reflection is an act of acceptance and healing for yourself.

Connecting with the good things

Every day, be aware of the beauty and wonder of life. Connect yourself to them and let them into you. The positive vitality of nature and the universe surrounds you. The beauty and soul of creation are all around you. If your life is stimulated purely by the stuff of human culture, you are missing the whole point. You are imprisoned in Blobsville. You can't take material success or status or any of that stuff with you! What matters is your health and integrity.

At least once a day, allow yourself to experience the reality of what is really there. It is not fair on yourself only to recognise the beauty of life a few times a year. You can't wait for your annual long holiday to remember what it is like to feel good. The vital and benevolent fields of energy are always there surrounding you. Just put in your plug and flick the switch.

It does not matter how you connect with the beauty of life.

Contemplative, ecstatic or devotee. On your knees in church. On your bike in the park. With your cat in front of the television. In an art gallery. At a soccer match. Dancing. Pausing. How you do it does not matter! Just do it. Every day, press the pause button on your remote control and change transmitters all together. Be aware of the Greater Life and allow yourself to feel and appreciate it.

You can also experiment with turning the volume up on this experience. Never take it for granted or become accustomed to it. Spend longer in the experience. Deepen the relationship. Be grateful. Then deepen it again. Brighten the colours, sounds, scents and feelings. Stretch the muscles of your spiritual awareness.

Doing good
You also have to do good. Doing good for others is the major external sign that you genuinely feel safe and great. Feeling safe and great without doing good may just be selfish or smug. Being tight with your resources – material and emotional – is a symptom of unhealthy blockage. It is really best to liberate yourself from this constriction, which is based in fear. Let your goodwill be felt by others.

The prime indicator of healthy energy is that it is flowing. Polluted rivers and lakes clean up miraculously fast when the water is allowed to flow. Your safety and your good feelings are also energies. They have to extend and flow beyond you. Do not clog up and become polluted.

Day by day you need to do good things. Minimally, at the end of any day, you should be able to look back and see at least one example of good and generous behaviour. It could be a specific event, like giving away some money with a genuine attitude of generosity or smiling at a stranger;

helping someone when the photocopying machine breaks down; being patient with an angry driver.

Or you can develop a more general attitude of generosity. In spiritual and religious circles, this is often described as developing your life to be of service. You can look at your life day by day and ask whether you are of service. Does your existence give anything to the world around you? You can spend some time every day in silent contemplation, sending love and tolerance into the world, breathing in negativity, breathing out blessing.

Some people may ask what it really means to be of service. I think the answer is simple. Everything in the cosmos is on a path of growth and fulfilment. Anything you do that supports growth and fulfilment is of service. Anything you do that blocks it is not of service.

Plants need water and sunshine to grow. More than anything else, people need safety and encouragement. So one easy way of monitoring whether you are of service and a positive benefit to the world is to assess whether you make people feel safe and encouraged. This may just be the matter of a smile; or it may mean extending your own sense of safety to include and hold others; or it may mean courageously countering abuse. You have also to appreciate how crucial your attitude and vibrations are; make sure you cause no harm and encourage and support the communities around you.

I fully appreciate that you may be living an intense 24/7 life. It may seem difficult to squeeze in the time, space and awareness to put these three practices into all your other demanding commitments. But why are you alive? Not to be the slave of a lifestyle. Feed yourself. Nurture your soul. Find balance.

Both when things are difficult for you and when they are going extremely well, your line to reality and to maintaining a safe centre may well be that of keeping to these three simple practices: *self-reflection, connecting with the good things* and *doing good.*

The Lion and the Sun

In these last pages, let us return to that beautiful creature, the lion, who has appeared several times in this book as an example of courage, strength and caring. In many fables, it is these attributes which lead to the lion being named king of the jungle, king of the beasts. This is a good metaphor for how a human being can behave in the jungle of life, as monarch of the beasts – the beasts within you and the beasts all around – courageous, strong and caring.

No wonder, then, that the lion is also found so often in heraldry, on shields and flags, symbolising regal strength and wisdom. This is an inspiring image – leadership with wise power. It is the absolute opposite of fear, anxiety and cowardice.

In some classical mythology the symbol of the idealised lion is given even more force. The images of the Sun and of the lion are merged into one figure. The countenance and golden mane of the lion become the face, halo and rays of the Sun. Here, the lion is a creature of almost limitless power, for the Sun never tires of radiating its energy, light and heat – an unending act of vital generosity which gives life. This is how to be a monarch – a person in whose aura people find life, health, growth and abundance.

But what a high ideal! What a romantic vision! Is it naive? Is it too high to achieve – this idea that you can be so strong and generous?

In the film *The Wizard of Oz* you may remember the timid and affectionate lion who accompanies Dorothy and her companions on her quest to find the Wizard. The lion is embarrassed because he has lost his courage and hopes that the Wizard will give it back to him. (The tin man wants a heart and the straw scarecrow wants a brain.)

Finally, they reach the Wizard, who tells the meek lion that he will find his courage only after he has confronted the Wicked Witch. The lion shudders at the mere idea of such a meeting. Nevertheless he accompanies Dorothy and circumstances unfold so that he does indeed confront the Witch and her terrible demons. He helps Dorothy and behaves with great courage.

The timid lion then returns to the Wizard in order to be given his reward, the courage that he so desperately wants. The Wizard says that he will not give it to him! He does not need to – because the lion has already found it! This is proved by the fact that he has already behaved bravely! The lion blushes cutely.

I like the story because it shows that the lion had never really lost his courage. It was always inside, waiting for the right time to emerge. Then, even after recognising that he was brave, he was still a guffawing and modest creature.

Sacrifice for the Community of Life

Courage and strength, although often hidden, are in all of us. They are built into you simply because you are alive. They are natural and normal. They are part of how our species survives and evolves. The otherwise meek parent suddenly roars with protective fury when a child is threatened. A teacher stands in the way of a madman when students are threatened. An unknown soldier stands in front of a comrade to take a bullet. A quiet priest walks first into the gas chamber ahead of the Jews. We all possess courage and strength, but how often do they emerge?

We are great souls, but we are also sensitive and frail mammals, like the monkeys I mentioned at the start of this book who were deprived of the warmth and care they needed in order to develop naturally and strongly. What a spectrum we represent: depth, wisdom and strength at one end – anxiety, fear and neurosis at the other. We are extraordinary and tragic. We are also just bumbling along as best we can.

But never forget that beneath that bumbling there is always the latent presence of your soul, your will to live and your connection with the power of all life. You do indeed possess courage, even if it is hidden – and remember that the definition of a brave person is someone who acts courageously even when they are experiencing fear.

Brought up by a perfect family in a perfect society, you would have no doubts about your safety and your courage. But life is tough and you will have taken some knocks – and you may therefore not be so sure about your inner strength. This lack of certainty is also normal. You may therefore want to build up your courage.

In some cultures, warriors work hard to build their mettle and prepare for the harsh realities of battle. Some go through ceremonies in which they voluntarily wound and scar themselves. By voluntarily experiencing pain and danger, they become oblivious to threat and hurl themselves into war.

In many religions, people also undergo voluntary suffering, but in a different way. They accept the pain and suffering of life with awareness and love. The death of Jesus is portrayed in Christianity as the supreme gesture of compassion and grace.

Within the ancient mystical schools of Europe this particular lesson of loving self-sacrifice was symbolised by the image of a pelican feeding its young with flesh torn from its own breast. This ideal of giving yourself for the service of others is also the core of chivalry in the great knightly orders – strength and courage developed only for the service of others.

There are many examples of this kind of compassionate courage. I am always deeply moved when I think of those priests who went into the Nazi concentration camps and voluntarily entered the gas chambers before their companions. While writing this book, I was also touched by the tragic story of a young woman with cancer who refused chemotherapy whilst pregnant, thus saving the life of her child but condemning herself. There was a photograph of her in the newspaper, smiling and with sparkling, joyful eyes, holding her newborn infant and surrounded by her family. Within a year of her child's birth, she died.

These are extreme instances, but they are inspiring. Yet again, we face the poignancy and paradox of the human condition – a recognition that true safety, generosity and courage may sometimes lead to self-sacrifice. It is an act that some people consciously and deliberately choose. And sometimes it may be unavoidable; circumstances force courage to emerge, as, for example, when your children are threatened.

This is a very sensitive area. On the one hand, I am encouraging you to take proper holistic care of yourself, to build your strength and sense of safety. On the other hand, there are risks because true safety manifests in goodwill to the community of life around you; sometimes that goodwill demands that you take courageous action and sacrifice yourself for others to make life better and safer for them. Only you can judge when this is right and when it is wrong.

There are always tiny gestures you can make, which will build strength of character and underpin your personal sense of security. There are always small sacrifices you can make:

- Allowing others to go first.

- Apologising.

- Giving money cheerfully.

- Giving time cheerfully.

- Containing your bad mood and being generous.

- Pausing to help.

- Making career choices that serve rather than suck.

- Paying more for ethically and environmentally sound products and services.

- Being open to changing your opinion.

- Opposing prejudice and racism.

- Listening carefully.

- Buying less and giving more.

- Encouraging others . . . and so on.

These actions may seem trivial compared to the great sacrifices of people who lay down their lives, but the tiniest act in the right direction is meaningful and useful – a million times better than no gesture at all. Moreover, these small acts exercise the muscles of your moral attitude, muscles that can later be used in more trying circumstances.

First Principles

In conclusion, let me remind you again of the true importance of feeling safe. Have no doubt about it. A sense of safety is the foundation for becoming a whole human being. As surely as you need food and shelter in order to live any kind of decent life, you also need to feel safe.

All the modern comforts and status in the world are meaningless if you do not feel safe. The chemistry of anxiety in your body will block you from feeling good. You may have occasional highs, but the rest of the time there will be a nagging irritation that everything could be so much better. And indeed it can be.

A genuine sense of safety, the ability to manage the threats and changes in life, creates a deep feeling of ease, stability and connection with the good things of life.

Throughout the book you have looked at how insecurity can sabotage your development and fulfilment, and your purpose as a human being. You absolutely owe it to yourself and to the community of life around you to create safety for yourself. You know that you cannot depend on the outside world for this security. It is great when external circumstances bring you safety, but it is naive to depend on it. The furies of nature and humanity may erupt anywhere and at any time, bringing tragedy and disaster. How will you be in those testing times?

It is wise to develop the safety within you, and you now have strategies that will help.

- *Press the pause button.*

- *Focus your caring mind down into yourself and manage your internal chemistry.*

- *Detach from the endless stimulation of human culture.*

- *Connect back with nature, the universe, with the good things of life.*

- *'Hold' any discomfort you may feel. Hold others in safety. Hold positive vision.*

- *Be aware of how energies and group histories can affect and influence you.*

- *Do not worry and radiate negative energy. It attracts what you do not want.*

- *Build clear boundaries.*

- *Be realistic about life and face the truth about yourself and the world.*

- *Breathe in negativity. Breathe out love.*

- *Create positive thoughts for troubled situations.*

- *Be courageous and generous.*

These strategies work and are easy because they are natural. They are the symptoms of a fulfilling and healthy life.

The six billion people on this Earth, the plants, animals and landscape, need you to feel safe and great. It is of no benefit to anyone or anything if you are insecure. The interdependence of all life demands that you accept your responsibility and your share of leadership. It starts with managing your own personal experience.

In the same way as a seed contains a tree, so within you there is already a true feeling of safety. Allow it to develop. This will bring you deep satisfaction and a genuine sense of fulfilment. The whole fellowship of life calls you to be like this and will benefit from your presence.

Resources

William Bloom PhD is considered by many to be Britain's leading holistic teacher. He cofounded Alternatives and is the founder of the educational consultancy Holistic Partnerships, which promotes his work in organisations as well as with individuals. For information on William Bloom's courses and other materials, please contact:

> Holistic Partnerships
> 10 The Murreys
> Ashtead
> Surrey KT21 2LU
> Tel: 01372 272400
> welcome@holisticpartnerships.com
> or visit **www.williambloom.com**

Other Relevant Books by William Bloom

The Endorphin Effect The revolutionary programme for successful self-development, health and healing.

Psychic Protection The bestselling classic on how to deal with negative energies and create a positive atmosphere.

Working with Angels, Fairies and Nature Spirits A wise and practical book on how to cooperate with these invisible realms – at home, at work, in the garden, in healing and in the arts.

The Penguin Book of New Age and Holistic Writing (Editor) A collection of the best and most inspiring material by the leading authors in the field.